Flash
Pocketbook

AS/A-Level Physics
Mechanics & Materials, Waves & Particles

Philip Allan Updates, an imprint of Hodder Education, an Hachette UK company, Market Place, Deddington, Oxfordshire OX15 0SE

Orders

Bookpoint Ltd, 130 Milton Park, Abingdon, Oxfordshire OX14 4SB
tel: 01235 827720   fax: 01235 400454   e-mail: uk.orders@bookpoint.co.uk

Lines are open 9.00 a.m.–5.00 p.m., Monday to Saturday, with a 24-hour message answering service. You can also order through our website: www.philipallan.co.uk

© Philip Allan Updates 2010
ISBN 978-1-4441-0909-2

First published in 2004 as *Flashrevise Cards*

Impression number 5 4 3 2 1
Year   2015   2014   2013   2012   2011   2010

Printed in Spain

Hachette UK's policy is to use papers that are natural, renewable and recyclable products and made from wood grown in sustainable forests. The logging and manufacturing processes are expected to conform to the environmental regulations of the country of origin.

P01640

Fundamentals
1 Fundamentals
2 Scalars and vectors
3 Vector calculations

Mechanics
4 Equations of motion
5 Dynamics
6 Conditions for equilibrium
7 Projectiles and free fall
8 Newton's first law
9 Newton's third law
10 Moments, torque and the principle of moments
11 Centre of gravity
12 Density
13 Pressure
14 Newton's second law and momentum
15 Collisions and impulse
16 Work, energy and power
17 Archimedes' principle and flotation
18 Drag and terminal velocity
19 Car safety
20 Law of conservation of energy
21 Energy from the environment I
22 Energy from the environment II

Radioactivity
23 Background radiation and ray properties
24 Uses of radioisotopes
25 Isotopes and nuclear equations I
26 Isotopes and nuclear equations II
27 Random decay
28 Nuclear stability
29 Exponential decay and half-life I
30 Exponential decay and half-life II
31 Experiments with radioactivity I
32 Experiments with radioactivity II

Particle Physics
33 Scattering experiments
34 Exchange particles
35 Nuclear forces
36 Composition of particles
37 Particles and anti-particles
38 Conservation laws in particle physics
39 Feynman diagrams

Electricity
40 Electric charge
41 Conduction in solids, liquids and gases
42 Ohm's law and I–V curves
43 Drift velocity of electrons
44 Metals, semiconductors and insulators I
45 Metals, semiconductors and insulators II
46 Resistivity
47 Effect of temperature and light on resistance
48 Electrical power
49 Kirchhoff's first and second laws
50 Ohm's law for a complete circuit

51 Internal resistance I
52 Internal resistance II
53 Resistors in series and parallel I
54 Resistors in series and parallel II
55 Potential dividers
56 DC circuit theory I
57 DC circuit theory II
58 AC circuit theory I
59 AC circuit theory II

Solid Materials
60 Hooke's law and spring constant
61 Stress–strain curves and Young's
   modulus I
62 Stress–strain curves and Young's
   modulus II
63 Work done in stretching wires
64 Ductility and brittleness
65 Structure of materials
66 Work hardening and annealing
67 Polymer and rubber properties
68 Composite materials

Waves
69 Wave motion I
70 Wave motion II
71 Wave speed
72 Phase difference and path difference
73 Electromagnetic waves
74 Plane polarisation of waves I
75 Plane polarisation of waves II

76 Inverse square law I
77 Inverse square law II
78 Wavefronts I
79 Wavefronts II
80 Principle of superposition
81 Stationary (standing) waves I
82 Stationary (standing) waves II
83 Stationary (standing) waves III
84 Young's slits experiment
85 Diffraction
86 Diffraction grating
87 Wave–particle duality
88 Photoelectric effect
89 Energy levels and line spectra
90 Reflection and refraction at a plane
   surface
91 Snell's law and refractive index
92 Total internal reflection and critical angle
93 Refraction through lenses
94 Sum over paths: theory
95 Sum over paths: applications
96 Digital imaging
97 Analogue and digital signals
98 Signal spectra and bandwidth

Experimental Method
99 Errors of observation and their
   treatment
100 Mathematical and graphical techniques

Fundamentals

Q1 What are the base quantities of physics? Give their units.

Q2 Give two examples of derived quantities and state their units.

Q3 What is meant by a homogeneous equation? Give an example, with an explanation, of a homogeneous equation that is nevertheless incorrect.

ANSWERS

A1 Mass, kg; length, m; time, s; current, A; temperature interval, K

A2 Velocity, $m\,s^{-1}$; density, $kg\,m^{-3}$

A3 One in which the units (or dimensions) are the same on both sides of the equation. An equation of this type might be $10\,N = 5\,N$. The dimensions are correct, but the magnitudes nevertheless are incorrect.

examiner's **note** Other base units are the mole (mol), the unit of quantity, and the candela (cd), the unit of luminous intensity. Other examples of derived quantities include force (N), acceleration ($m\,s^{-2}$) and pressure or stress (Pa). When checking dimensional homogeneity, use units, rather than physical quantities. Another example of this type of (incorrect) equation is kinetic energy = $2mv^2$.

Scalars and vectors

Q1 Explain the difference between scalars and vectors.

Q2 Classify the following as scalars or vectors: mass, acceleration, force, density, momentum, power, displacement, temperature, work, energy, time, distance, speed, weight, velocity.

Q3 A train changes its velocity from $3.0\,\mathrm{m\,s^{-1}}$ due east to $2.5\,\mathrm{m\,s^{-1}}$ due south. Calculate its change in (a) speed and (b) velocity.

ANSWERS

A1 Scalars have magnitude only; vectors have direction as well as magnitude

A2 Scalars: mass, density, power, temperature, work, energy, time, distance, speed

Vectors: acceleration, force, momentum, displacement, weight, velocity

A3 (a) Change in speed = 2.5 − 3.0 = −0.5 m s^{-1}. You can use simple subtraction because speed is a scalar quantity.

(b) Since velocity is a vector, we have to use a vector triangle (using Pythagoras' theorem), i.e. change in velocity = $\sqrt{2.5^2 + 3.0^2}$ = 3.9 m s^{-1}

***examiner's* note** You should be familiar with most physical quantities and know whether they are vectors or scalars.

Vector calculations

Q1 A person walks 3.0 m due north, followed by 4.0 m due east. Find the magnitude and direction of the person's displacement.

Q2 Find the magnitude and direction of the resultant of forces of 2 N and 3 N acting so that there is an angle of 60° between them.

ANSWERS

A1 $s^2 = 3^2 + 4^2$, giving $x = 5.0\,\text{m}$ at an angle θ of $\tan^{-1}(4/3)$, giving $\theta = 53.1°$

A2 Apply the cosine rule:
$OC^2 = CB^2 + OB^2 - (2CB \times OB \cos OBC)$.
$OBC = 180° - AOB = 120°$ so $OC^2 = 19$ and $OC = \sqrt{19} = 4.4\,\text{N}$

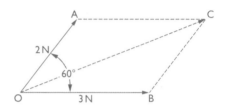

Apply the sine rule:
$2/\sin COB = 4.4/\sin 120°$, giving angle $COB = 23°24'$.

***examiner's* note** In question 1 the vectors are at right angles so we may use Pythagoras' theorem to solve for the magnitude of the displacement. Basic trigonometry gives the angle of inclination of the particular vector. In question 2 a scale drawing could also be used to solve the problem.

Equations of motion

Q1 What are the four main equations of uniformly accelerated linear motion?

Q2 What is the physical significance of (a) the gradient of an s–t graph; (b) the gradient of a v–t graph; (c) the area under a v–t graph; (d) a curved v–t graph?

Q3 Starting from $s = \frac{1}{2}(u + v)t$ and $v = u + at$, show that $v^2 = u^2 + 2as$.

ANSWERS ▶▶

A1 • $v = u + at$
   • $s = ut + \frac{1}{2}at^2$
   • $v^2 = u^2 + 2as$
   • $s = \frac{1}{2}(u + v)t$

A2 (a) Velocity at that point (b) Acceleration at that point
   (c) Total displacement (d) Non-constant acceleration

A3 $v = u + at$, so $(v - u)/a = t$
   Substituting $(v - u)/a = t$ in $s = \frac{1}{2}(u + v)t$: $s = \frac{1}{2}(u + v)(v - u)/a$.
   Rearranging: $2as = (u + v)(v - u)$
   so $v^2 - u^2 = 2as$, which gives $v^2 = u^2 + 2as$

***examiner's* note** You should know these equations and how to use them.
You should be fully conversant with all these types of graph and realise that for
free-fall, the a–t graph is a straight line, parallel to the t-axis.

Dynamics

Q1 A train with velocity $5.0\,\mathrm{m\,s^{-1}}$ accelerates uniformly at $2.0\,\mathrm{m\,s^{-2}}$ for $10\,\mathrm{s}$. Calculate (a) the final velocity and (b) the distance travelled.

Q2 A car, starting from rest, reaches a speed of $16\,\mathrm{m\,s^{-1}}$ in $8\,\mathrm{s}$, travels at that speed for $20\,\mathrm{s}$ and then slows down uniformly to rest in $10\,\mathrm{s}$. Find the distance travelled.

Q3 A cricket ball is thrown vertically upwards with a velocity of $20\,\mathrm{m\,s^{-1}}$. Calculate (a) the maximum height reached and (b) the time taken to return to the ground. Neglect air resistance ($g = 10\,\mathrm{m\,s^{-2}}$).

ANSWERS

A1 (a) $v = u + at$, $v = 5.0 + (2.0 \times 10) = 25\,\text{m s}^{-1}$

(b) $s = ut + \frac{1}{2}at^2 = (5.0 \times 10) + \frac{1}{2} \times 2.0 \times (10)^2 = 150\,\text{m}$

A2 The distance travelled by a body = area under velocity–time graph. In this case, it consists of 2 triangles and 1 rectangle. During 0–8 s, distance travelled = $\frac{1}{2} \times 8 \times 16 = 64\,\text{m}$; 8–28 s, distance = $(20 \times 16) = 320\,\text{m}$; 28–38 s, distance = $\frac{1}{2} \times 16 \times 10 = 80\,\text{m}$. So, total distance travelled = $64 + 320 + 80 = 464\,\text{m}$.

A3 Taking upwards as positive, $u = +20\,\text{m s}^{-1}$; $a = g = -10\,\text{m s}^{-2}$

(a) Use $v^2 = u^2 + 2as$; at the maximum height, $v = 0$. Thus, $(0)^2 = (20)^2 + 2(-10)s$, giving $s = 20\,\text{m}$.

(b) On its return to the ground, the displacement $s = 0$, giving $s = ut + \frac{1}{2}at^2$, which gives $0 = 20t - \frac{1}{2} \times 10 \times t^2$, which gives $t = 4.0\,\text{s}$.

***examiner's* note** When dealing with vertical motion (as in question 3), adopt a sign convention. Usually, this is 'upwards is positive', which gives $g = -10\,\text{m s}^{-2}$.

5 **ANSWERS**

Conditions for equilibrium

Q1 State the triangle of forces theorem for three non-parallel forces acting on an object.

Q2 What are the two conditions for a rigid body to be in equilibrium under a set of forces?

Q3 A horizontal force F is applied to a mass m on a smooth plane at an angle θ to the horizontal. The condition for equilibrium is:

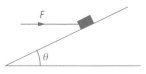

A $F \cos \theta - mg \sin \theta = 0$
B $F \sin \theta + mg \cos \theta = 0$
C $F \cos \theta + mg \sin \theta = 0$
D $F \sin \theta - mg \cos \theta = 0$

ANSWERS

A1 If three forces are in equilibrium, they can be represented in magnitude and direction by the three sides of a triangle taken in order.

A2 The algebraic sum of the moments of all the forces about any point is zero and the algebraic sum of the resolved components of all the forces in any direction is zero.

A3 Only A is correct.

***examiner's* note** The component of the object's weight parallel to and down the plane is $mg \sin \theta$. The component of F parallel to the plane is $F \cos \theta$ up the plane.

Projectiles and free fall

Q1 What factors affect the range (horizontal distance) of a projectile? Give (a) one benefit and (b) one disadvantage of using a large distance in a free-fall experiment to find g.

Q2 In an experiment to measure the acceleration of free fall, a steel ball took 571 ms to fall a distance of 1.60 m from rest. Calculate a value for the acceleration of free fall.

Q3 A tennis ball passes horizontally just over the net and lands just inside the baseline of the court. The net has a height of 1.07 m and is 11.9 m from the baseline. Find the horizontal speed of the tennis ball. Ignore air resistance and spin; take g as 9.81 m s^{-2}.

ANSWERS

A1 Launch angle, launch velocity, value of g
(a) Greater distance implies less error in measurements of both time and distance (b) Longer distances mean greater drag, leading to longer times and giving a lower value than expected for g

A2 Use $s = ut + \frac{1}{2}gt^2$, where $s = 1.60\,\text{m}$; $u = 0\,\text{m s}^{-1}$; $t = 0.571\,\text{s}$. This gives $g = 9.81\,\text{m s}^{-2}$.

A3 Use vertical motion to find the time in the air, where $u = 0\,\text{m s}^{-1}$; $s = 1.07\,\text{m}$; $a = g = 9.81\,\text{m s}^{-2}$. Using the equation, $s = ut + \frac{1}{2}at^2$, gives $t = 0.47\,\text{s}$. Horizontal speed is given by $v = s/t = 11.9/0.47 = 25.3\,\text{m s}^{-1}$.

***examiner's* note** Since time is proportional to the square root of distance, a suitably wide range of distances should be selected to avoid 'cramming' of results. Projectile motion is dealt with by separating vertical and horizontal motions. Time spent in the air is calculated from free-fall data. Horizontal displacement is found from distance = speed × time, assuming negligible air resistance.

 ANSWERS

Newton's first law

Q1 State Newton's first law of motion.

Q2 Name the four principal types of force in physics. Distinguish between contact and non-contact forces. Give examples of each.

Q3 What conditions are necessary for a body to be at its terminal velocity?

ANSWERS

A1 A body remains at rest or at uniform velocity in a straight line unless acted upon by a force

A2 Gravitational, electric, magnetic and nuclear. Contact forces exist between bodies that are very close together. Non-contact forces, as their name implies, act at a distance. Examples of contact forces include normal reaction, air resistance (drag) and viscous forces. Non-contact forces are gravitational, electrostatic and magnetic.

A3 The resultant acceleration/force on it must be zero

***examiner's* note** Newton's first law introduces the concepts of force and inertia. Inertia is the resistance of a body at rest to movement and its reluctance to cease movement once movement has begun. Nuclear forces overcome the electrostatic repulsion of protons in the nucleus. Examples of bodies moving at terminal velocity are parachutes, raindrops and ball bearings moving under gravity in a viscous liquid in a tall jar — all after some time.

Newton's third law

Q1 State Newton's third law of motion. Give examples of Newton's third-law pairs of forces.

Q2 What five features must be present in a Newton's third-law pair of forces?

Q3 Explain the differences between Newton's first and third laws.

ANSWERS

A1 Action and reaction are equal and opposite. Examples: a planet pulls the Sun, and the Sun pulls the planet with an equal-sized force. In the case of a book resting on a table, we can say 'push of book on table equals push of table on book'. Alternatively, we may write 'pull of Earth on book equals pull of book on Earth'.

A2 The same type of force must be acting, the forces must be in opposite directions, they must act on different bodies, be equal in magnitude and act in the same line

A3 Newton's third law always applies; Newton's first law applies only to equilibrium situations. Newton's third law is about a pair of forces on two different bodies; Newton's first law is about the forces acting on a single body. Newton's third law applies to two forces only; Newton's first law applies to any number of forces.

***examiner's* note** When explaining Newton's third-law pairs of forces, do not mix the types of force involved.

 ANSWERS

Moments, torque and the principle of moments

Q1 State the principle of moments. What is the SI unit of moment?

Q2 A cyclist turns a corner by applying equal but opposite forces of 15 N to the ends of the handlebars of length 0.6 m. Calculate the torque applied to the handlebars.

Q3 A heavy uniform plank of length L is supported by two forces F_1 and F_2 at points $L/8$ and $L/4$ from its end. What is the ratio of F_1 to F_2?

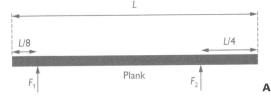

ANSWERS

A1 At equilibrium, the sum of the anticlockwise moments equals the sum of the clockwise moments, taken about any point. The SI unit of moment is $N\,m$.

A2 Torque = $15 \times 0.6 = 9\,N\,m$

A3 If the weight of the plank is W, then taking moments about the centre gives $F_1 \times 3L/8 = F_2 \times L/4$, so $F_1/F_2 = 2/3$.

examiner's note We take moments about the centre because we only want to find the ratio of the forces. Otherwise, we normally take moments about one of the support points to eliminate the unknown force there.

Centre of gravity

Q1 What is meant by (a) centre of mass; (b) centre of gravity?

Q2 How would you find the centre of gravity of a flat, irregular lamina? What unusual feature might there be about the centre of gravity of a body?

Q3 A rod of negligible mass and of length 3 m has masses at each end of 1 kg and 2 kg respectively. Where is the centre of mass?

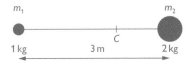

ANSWERS ▶▶

a) The point at which an applied force produces an acceleration, but no rotation. (b) The point at which the weight of a body acts or appears to act.

A2 Using a plumb-line, suspend the lamina from one point. Mark the line. Re-suspend from a different point, re-mark. Where the lines intersect is the centre of gravity. Unusual feature: centre of gravity may lie outside the body itself.

A3 Let the centre of gravity, C, lie x metres from the 2 kg mass. Taking moments about C: $1(3 - x) = 2x$, giving $x = 1$ m.

***examiner's* note** The centre of gravity usually lies inside the body. Exceptions include the human body (where use is made of this by divers and gymnasts), 'L'-shaped pieces of wire, life-belts/Polo mints/rings etc. In the case of circular objects, their centres of gravity lie at the centre of the circles.

(11) **ANSWERS**

Density

Q1 Define density and give its SI unit.

Q2 What physical conditions must be stated when quoting the density of (a) solids, (b) liquids, (c) gases?

Q3 An oil pipeline has a cylindrical cross-section of diameter 0.8 m. Oil flows through it at an average speed of 0.3 m s^{-1}. Calculate the average mass of oil flowing per second (density of oil = 800 kg m^{-3}).

ANSWERS

A1 Density = mass/volume; SI units: $kg\ m^{-3}$

A2 (a) None (b) Temperature only (c) Temperature and pressure

A3 Volume per second = $V = \pi r^2 v = \pi(0.4)^2 \times 0.3 = 0.151\ m^3\ s^{-1}$.
Since $m = V\rho$, mass per second = $0.151 \times 800 = 120.6\ kg\ s^{-1}$.

***examiner's* note** You should be familiar with the order of magnitudes of densities of common substances, such as air, water, and metals.

Pressure

Q1 Define pressure. What are its SI units?

Q2 The maximum pressure that human lungs can withstand is about 11 kPa. Approximately how deep in water can a diver go with a snorkel tube? ($g = 9.81\,\mathrm{m\,s^{-2}}$, $\rho = 1000\,\mathrm{kg\,m^{-3}}$)

Q3 A hydraulic jack consists of two pistons A and B of cross-sectional areas 25 cm^2 and 2000 cm^2 respectively. A load of 500 N is placed on A. (a) Calculate the pressure of oil in the system; (b) calculate the upward force on B.

ANSWERS

A1 Pressure = force/area; SI unit: $N\,m^{-2}$ or Pascal (Pa)

A2 $p = g\rho h$, giving $h = p/\rho g = (11 \times 10^3)/(1000 \times 9.81) = 1.1\,m$ (approx.)

A3 (a) Pressure = 500/25 = $20\,N\,cm^{-2}$

    (b) Force = pressure × area = $20 \times 2000 = 40\,000\,N$

***examiner's* note** In hydraulic systems, such as car brakes, air bubbles are undesirable because, unlike a liquid, the air in the bubbles can be compressed, lowering the effective pressure and resulting in 'spongy' brakes.

Newton's second law and momentum

Q1 State Newton's second law of motion. What experimental graphs are needed to verify Newton's second law?

Q2 A car pulls a caravan of mass 2000 kg along rough horizontal ground. The car exerts a force of 1000 N on the caravan, which accelerates at $0.20\,\text{m s}^{-2}$. What is the frictional force between the caravan and the ground?

Q3 (a) What is the expression for momentum? (b) What are its SI units? (c) State the principle of conservation of linear momentum. (d) A ball with momentum p strikes a wall and rebounds off it along the same line at the same speed. What is the change in the ball's momentum?

ANSWERS ▶▶

rate of change of momentum is directly proportional to the applied force and takes place in the same direction. Graphs are force versus acceleration and acceleration versus (1/mass).

A2 Let the resultant force be F. $F = ma$, so $F = 2000 \times 0.2 = 400\,N$. Since resultant force = pull of car − friction, it follows that $400 = 1000$ − friction, giving friction = $600\,N$.

A3 (a) mass × velocity (b) $kg\,m\,s^{-1}$ or $N\,s$ (c) The total momentum in a given direction of a system of colliding bodies remains constant, before and after a collision, providing no external forces act (d) $2p$

***examiner's* note** Newton's second-law experiment shows $F = k \times ma$. In the SI system, the constant k was chosen to be 1. Since momentum is a vector, direction needs to be specified. In question 3, the change in momentum = $p − (−p) = 2p$.

Collisions and impulse

Q1 (a) What is the difference between elastic and inelastic collisions? Give an example of each type. (b) Give two examples of recoil situations. What assumption needs to be made in order to solve recoil problems?

Q2 A cricket ball of mass 0.16 kg is moving at 50 m s⁻¹ and is caught by a fielder who brings it to rest in 0.1 s. Calculate the average force exerted by the fielder on the ball.

Q3 A tennis ball of mass 0.07 kg reaches a racket at a speed of 20 m s⁻¹ and leaves it at 10 m s⁻¹ in the opposite direction. The ball is in contact with the racket for 0.15 s. What is (a) the change of momentum and (b) the impulse given to the ball?

ANSWERS

A1 (a) In an elastic collision, the total kinetic energy (KE) of a system of colliding bodies remains constant. In inelastic collisions, such as a dynamics trolley colliding with another carrying a lump of Blu-tack, some KE is lost as heat or sound. An example of a perfectly elastic collision is a gas molecule colliding with the walls of its container. (b) Examples: nucleus splitting up in radioactive decay or the recoil of a gun. Assumption: total momentum = zero before and after the event.

A2 $F = \dfrac{mv - mu}{t}$; $F = \dfrac{(0.16 \times 0) - (0.16 \times 50)}{0.1}$, giving $F = -80\,\text{N}$

A3 (a) change in momentum $= mv - mu = m(v - u)$
$$= 0.07 \times (10 - (-20)) = -2.1\,\text{N s}$$
(b) impulse = change of momentum, so this is also $-2.1\,\text{N s}$

***examiner's* note** Momentum is conserved in all collisions. Total kinetic energy is conserved only in elastic collisions. Any collision in which the bodies stick together must be inelastic. Note the negative sign in answers 2 and 3: this indicates that the direction of the final force is opposite to its original path.

Work, energy and power

Q1 Define mechanical work and power. Give their SI units.

Q2 A ball of mass 0.45 kg falls from rest at a height of 45 m. Calculate (a) its original gravitational potential energy, (b) its final kinetic energy and (c) its final velocity. Neglect air resistance (take g as $10 \, m \, s^{-2}$).

Q3 An elastic band is pulled out steadily through a small distance of 1 cm and the force exerted increases steadily from 0 N to 10 N. Calculate the work done. Assume Hooke's law is obeyed.

ANSWERS

A1 Mechanical work done is the product of the average force and distance (or displacement) moved in the direction of the force; unit is joule (J). Power is the rate of working (work done divided by the time taken); unit is watt (W).

A2 (a) gravitational potential energy (GPE) = $mg\Delta h$ = 0.45 × 10 × 45 = 202.5 J (b) Assuming no air resistance, it follows that kinetic energy (KE) is equal to the initial GPE, i.e. 202.5 J (c) KE = $\frac{1}{2}mv^2$, giving 202.5 = $\frac{1}{2}$ × (0.45)v^2. This gives v = 30.0 m s^{-1}.

A3 Since force is proportional to the extension of the band, work done = average force × extension = $\frac{1}{2}$ × (0 + 10) × 0.01 = 0.05 J.

***examiner's* note** The law of conservation of energy can only be applied to problems in which no frictional forces act, such as air resistances or contact friction, e.g. a body moving on a rough table or bench.

Archimedes' principle and flotation

Q1 State Archimedes' principle.

Q2 A glass stopper is weighed in air then totally immersed in water and reweighed. The readings obtained were 2.4 N in air and 2.0 N in water. Given that the density of water is $1000 \, kg \, m^{-3}$, calculate the density of the stopper.

Q3 A block of cedar wood has a mass of 200 kg and a density of $570 \, kg \, m^{-3}$. What fraction of the wood will be under the surface when the block is floating in water? (Assume $g = 10 \, m \, s^{-2}$; density of water = $1000 \, kg \, m^{-3}$.)

ANSWERS))

A1 A body that is wholly or partially immersed in a fluid experiences an upthrust equal to the weight of fluid displaced.

A2 Weight of water displaced = 0.4 N, so mass of water displaced = 0.04 kg. Therefore the volume of water displaced = mass of water displaced/density of water = 0.04/1000 m^3 = volume of stopper. The mass of the stopper = 0.24 kg since its weight is 2.4 N. Density of the stopper = mass/volume = 0.24/(0.04/1000) = 6000 $kg\,m^{-3}$.

A3 Mass of water displaced = 200 kg. Volume displaced = mass/density = 200/1000 = 0.20 m^3. Volume = mass/density = 200/570 = 0.351 m^3. Proportion of wood submerged = 0.200/0.351 = 0.57.

***examiner's* note** In question 3, the wood will float when it displaces a weight of water equal to its own weight.

Drag and terminal velocity

Q1 What conditions cause a terminal velocity to be attained?

Q2 Sketch a graph showing how the velocity changes with time for an object falling through water.

Q3 A drop of radius r is falling through air of density ρ and viscosity η at a speed v. Using dimensional analysis, the resistive force F on the drop *might* be proportional to which one or more of the following?

A $r\rho v$ B $r^2\rho v^2$ C $r^2\eta v^2$ D $r\eta v$

ANSWERS 〉〉

A1 Terminal velocity is attained when the resultant force on the body is zero. Diagram (i) illustrates this point: at the terminal velocity, $F + U = mg$

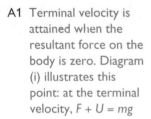

A2 The sketch graph required in response to question 2 is shown in diagram (ii).

A3 B and D are correct.

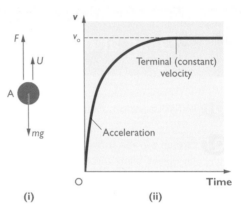

(i)   (ii)

examiner's **note** In question 1 terminal velocity is reached when the weight of the object (mg) is equal to the total upward forces acting — namely fluid friction or drag (F) plus any Archimedean upthrust forces acting (U), so $F + U = mg$. In question 3 the dimensions of η can be found from Stokes' law, $F = 6\pi\eta rv$.

Car safety

Q1 What factors affect thinking distance?

Q2 What factors affect braking distance?

Q3 Describe how airbags are triggered to inflate when a car is in a collision.

ANSWERS

A1 Speed and reaction time (the latter being affected by tiredness, illness and distractions).

A2 Braking distance depends on the braking force, friction between the tyres and the road, the mass and the speed.

A3 Airbags are triggered to inflate using sensors that detect the rapid deceleration of a car in a crash.

examiner's note Thinking distance = speed × reaction time. Braking force is reduced by reduced friction between the brakes and the wheels (worn or defective brakes).

Friction between the tyres and the road is reduced by wet or icy roads, worn tyres etc. Mass depends on the size of car and its loading.

To trigger the airbags, most cars use a microchip accelerometer, which in turn sends a signal to the airbag modules in the car.

Law of conservation of energy

Q1 State the law of conservation of energy.

Q2 A bullet, X, of mass 50 g
(0.05 kg) is fired with a
velocity of 100 m s⁻¹ into a
stationary block of mass 2 kg
suspended at the end of a
long string. Calculate the
height to which the block
rises if the bullet becomes
embedded in the block.

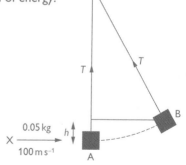

ANSWERS

A1 The total energy in a closed (isolated) system stays constant though this energy can change from one form to another.

A2 Initial momentum of bullet = final momentum of (block + bullet)

So, $0.05 \times 100 = (2.0 + 0.05)v_{final}$, giving $v_{final} = 2.44 \text{ m s}^{-1}$.
By conservation of energy, $\frac{1}{2}mv_{final}^2 = mgh$, so $\frac{1}{2} \times 2.05 \times (2.44)^2 = 2.05 \times 9.81 \times h$, giving $h = 0.30 \text{ m}$

***examiner's* note** When answering question 3 use the conservation of momentum first to find the velocity of the block and bullet, since this is an inelastic collision.

Energy from the environment I

Q1 A windmill for a power source sweeps out an area of 20 m diameter. If 60% of the available energy is converted into energy, calculate the power produced in a wind of velocity 13 m s⁻¹.

Q2 In a tidal power system, the water is trapped in a basin of 40 km² and the maximum height of water is 10 m. If the time from high to low tides is 6 hours, calculate the average power output.

Q3 Estimate the power output per km of a wave-power system. Assume rectangular waves with wavefronts 1 m wide, amplitude 1 m and wavelength 100 m, with a 5 s periodic time. (Assume $g = 10$ m s⁻², density of water = 1000 kg m⁻³, density of air = 1.3 kg m⁻³.)

ANSWERS ▶▶

A1 The cylindrical column of air moving to the circular area of the rotating blade in 1 s has a volume $= \pi \times 10^2 \times 13 = 4084\,m^3$.
Mass of air reaching the blade per second $= 4084 \times 1.3 = 5300\,kg$ (approx.). Kinetic energy per second of the air $= \frac{1}{2}mv^2 = \frac{1}{2} \times 5300 \times (13)^2 = 0.45$ MW. At 60% efficiency, this gives 0.27 MW.

A2 Weight of water, mg = volume × density × g
$$= 40 \times 10^6 \times 1000 \times 10 = 4 \times 10^{11}\,N$$
Change in GPE $= mg \times h/2 = 4 \times 10^{11} \times 10/2 = 2 \times 10^{12}\,J$
Therefore, average power $= (2 \times 10^{12})/(6 \times 3600) = 90$ MW

A3 Mass of water = volume × density $= (50 \times 1 \times 1) \times 1000$
$$= 5 \times 10^4\,kg$$
Change in GPE of water $= mg\Delta h = 5 \times 10^4 \times 10 \times 1 = 5 \times 10^5\,J$.
So, power = energy/time $= 10^5/5 = 20\,000$ W. For a 1 km or 1000 m wavefront, power $= 1000 \times 20$ kW $= 20$ MW.

***examiner's* note** In question 2, if the maximum height of water above low tide is h, the centre of gravity is at a height $h/2$ above low tide.

Energy from the environment II

Q1 The reservoir for a HEP station is 40 m above the turbines. If the overall efficiency of the station is 50%, what mass of water must flow through the turbines per second to generate 1 MW of power? (Assume $g = 10\,\mathrm{m\,s^{-2}}$, density of water = $1000\,\mathrm{kg\,m^{-3}}$.)

Q2 Taking the solar constant as $1.4\,\mathrm{kW\,m^{-2}}$ and assuming a reduction of 50% by atmospheric absorption, calculate the total solar energy arriving at the Earth's surface in an hour. Radius of Earth = 6400 km. (Allow for day and night and that not all the Earth's surface is normal to the radiation.)

Q3 Name two types of energy that may be regarded as not derived from the Sun.

ANSWERS

A1 Change in GPE/s = mgh = 1 000 000 J. So, $m \times 10 \times 40$ = 1 000 000, giving m = 1 000 000/400 = 2500 kg. But the plant is 50% efficient, giving m = 5000 kg every second.

A2 Actual power = 700 W. Accounting for night and day, this becomes 350 W.
Hence, energy per hour = $\pi (6400 \times 10^3)^2 \times 350 \times 60 \times 60$
$$= 1.62 \times 10^{20} \text{ J}.$$

A3 Geothermal and nuclear

examiner's note In question 2, assume the Earth to be a flat, circular disc, always having the Sun's rays falling on it.

Background radiation and ray properties

Q1 Give two sources of natural background radiation.

Q2 What is the general relationship between ionising power and penetration range?

Q3 What is the SI unit of radioactive disintegration rate?

ANSWERS

A1 Cosmic rays from outer space and rocks (uranium ore). Before any experiment involving radioactivity is carried out, the 'background count' must be measured using a Geiger–Müller tube and counter.

A2 More strongly ionising power implies that the range is shorter

A3 The becquerel (Bq) = 1 disintegration per second

examiner's note Ancient igneous rocks, e.g. granite, are rich sources of radon gas. Energy is absorbed by the matter through which the ionising rays pass, e.g. air molecules. In base units the becquerel is s^{-1}.

Uses of radioisotopes

Q1 Explain how smoke detectors work.

Q2 Explain why beta emitters, rather than alpha or gamma emitters, are used in paper mills to measure the thickness of paper.

Q3 Explain why gamma emitters are preferred over alpha or beta emitters for medical treatment and diagnosis.

ANSWERS ▶▶

A1 Alpha radiation falls from a source on a detector, giving rise to a small current. Output is off and the alarm is silent. When smoke enters the gap, it absorbs the radiation. Because no current flows, the alarm is sounded.

A2 Beta radiation is used for this application since alpha radiation would be absorbed entirely by the paper. Gamma radiation would hardly be affected, since it is the most penetrating.

A3 Alpha rays have virtually no penetrating power; beta rays, although penetrating, are only moderately ionising

***examiner's* note** Highly ionising radiations are dangerous to human health since they cause cell mutation and damage. It is this cell damage that is used in medical applications, when gamma rays are used to kill tumour cells.

Isotopes and nuclear equations I

Q1 What is meant by the term 'isotope'? Why are the chemical properties of isotopes identical?

Q2 What are the usual symbols for (a) an alpha particle, (b) a beta-minus particle, (c) a gamma ray, (d) a proton, (e) a neutron and (f) a positron?

Q3 When writing nuclear equations, which three items must be conserved?

ANSWERS

A1 Isotopes are atoms of the same element that differ only in the number of neutrons in their nuclei. Their chemical properties are identical since it is the outer electrons that determine chemical properties.

A2 (a) $_2^4\text{He}^{2+}$ (b) $_{-1}^{0}\text{e}^{-}$ (c) $_0^0\gamma$ (d) $_1^1\text{H}^{+}$ (e) $_0^1\text{n}$ (f) $_{+1}^{0}\text{e}^{+}$

A3 Mass number, proton number, mass–energy

***examiner's* note** The physical properties of isotopes, e.g. boiling point and density, differ since their nuclei have different masses. This is used to separate them, e.g. gaseous diffusion or mass spectrometry. Mass–energy changes are not always obvious when balancing nuclear equations. Rather than using the (fractional) mass numbers, whole numbers are quoted for simplification.

Isotopes and nuclear equations II

Q1 Complete the following nuclear equation: $^{63}_{28}Ni = X + ^{63}_{29}Cu$.

Q2 When iron is irradiated with neutrons, a small proportion of a stable isotope $^{58}_{26}Fe$ becomes $^{59}_{26}Fe$. $^{59}_{26}Fe$ decays into (stable) $^{59}_{27}Co$. Write down the equation that represents the neutron absorption reaction by $^{58}_{26}Fe$.

Q3 Write down the equation for the decay of $^{58}_{26}Fe$ into $^{59}_{27}Co$ (stable).

ANSWERS ▶▶

A1 X is a beta-minus particle, $_{-1}^{0}e$

A2 $_{26}^{58}Fe + _{0}^{1}n = _{26}^{59}Fe$

A3 $_{26}^{59}Fe = _{27}^{59}Co + _{-1}^{0}e$

***examiner's* note** One application of the decay process shown in question 3 is in monitoring engine wear. You measure the increase in radioactivity of the engine oil after a period of time following the insertion of a disc of the iron-59 isotope in the cylinder of the engine.

Random decay

Q1 What is meant by random decay?

Q2 How could you demonstrate experimentally that radioactive decay is a random process?

Q3 What graph needs to be plotted to show stability/instability of isotopes?

ANSWERS ▶▶

A1 There is no way of predicting when a particular nucleus will decay

A2 Activity–time plots show slight fluctuations from ideal exponential decay

A3 Number of protons (x-axis) versus number of neutrons (y-axis)

examiner's note In a plot of activity versus time, statistically, the exponential decay law is obeyed. However, there may be several occasions when no decay occurs. Then, at another time, several decays may occur simultaneously.

Nuclear stability

These questions refer to the graph in question 3, Topic 27, plotted to show stability/instability of isotopes.

Q1 In what direction does a nucleus need to move to achieve greater stability by alpha emission?

Q2 In what direction does a nucleus need to move to achieve greater stability by beta (minus) emission?

Q3 In what direction does a nucleus need to move to achieve greater stability by positron emission?

ANSWERS

A1 'Southwest' (downwards towards the origin, 2 units down, 2 units to the left)

A2 'Southeast' (diagonally downwards towards the trend line, 1 unit down, 1 unit to the right)

A3 'Northwest' (diagonally upwards towards the trend line, 1 unit up, 1 unit to the left)

***examiner's* note** Alpha decay involves both proton and neutron numbers decreasing by two. Beta (minus) decay involves the neutron number decreasing by one and the proton number increasing by one. Positron decay involves the proton number decreasing by one and the neutron number increasing by one.

Exponential decay and half-life I

Q1 What is meant by exponential decay?

Q2 What is meant by the half-life of a radioisotope?

Q3 Define the radioactive decay constant and give its SI unit. Explain its relationship to (a) half-life and (b) number of radioactive nuclei present.

ANSWERS))

A1 The rate of disintegration is proportional to the number of radioactive nuclei present

A2 Half-life is the average time taken for the activity of a sample of a radioisotope to fall to one-half of its original value

A3 The radioactive decay constant is the probability that a nucleus will decay in a certain time. SI unit is s^{-1}.

(a) $\lambda = \dfrac{\ln 2}{t_{\frac{1}{2}}}$

(b) activity = $dN/dt = -\lambda N$ where N equals the number of undecayed radioactive atoms

***examiner's* note** When carrying out calculations involving activity and the number of nuclei present, remember that λ must have units of s^{-1}.

Exponential decay and half-life II

Q1 Carbon-14 has a half-life of 5730 years. If an archaeological sample has an activity of 7.5 disintegrations per minute, and an equal mass of carbon taken from a living plant has an activity of 15 disintegrations per minute, what is the age of the sample?

Q2 Why is it not possible to date precisely material that has been dead for more than about 12 000 years using carbon dating?

Q3 0.3619 mg sample of a radioisotope has an activity of 4.011×10^{12} Bq. If its molar mass is 218 g mol^{-1}, what is its half-life?

ANSWERS

A1 Since the activity has halved, it follows that the age of the sample is one half-life, i.e. 5730 years

A2 The activity of the sample becomes too low for precise analysis

A3 Number of moles in sample = $0.3619 \times 10^{-3}/218 = 1.66 \times 10^{-6}$.
Number of atoms = $6.02 \times 10^{23} \times 1.66 \times 10^{-6} = 1.0 \times 10^{18}$.
Activity = $-\lambda N$, giving $\lambda = (4.011 \times 10^{12})/1.0 \times 10^{18} = 4.011 \times 10^{-6}$.
But $\lambda = \ln 2/t_{\frac{1}{2}}$, giving $t_{\frac{1}{2}} = 1.72 \times 10^{5}$ s (or 2.00 days).

examiner's note Carbon dating is also imprecise for dating objects of plant or animal origin less than 1000 years old, since its activity is too close to that of living matter. The activity over an entire spherical surface is calculated by proportion, considering the area of the Geiger–Müller tube window and using the distance between the point source and the Geiger–Müller tube to work out the surface area of the sphere.

Experiments with radioactivity I

Q1 What precautions should be taken when handling radioisotopes?

Q2 What should be done first before carrying out any experiment involving radioactivity?

Q3 The table shows the count rate (with and without a source) at various times. What is the half-life of the source?

Time/days	Count rate with source (Bq)	Count rate without source
20	120	40
60	60	40
120	42	40

ANSWERS ▶▶

A1 The source must be handled with long tongs. Keep the source in a lead box until required. After the experiment, replace the source in a lead box.

A2 Using a Geiger–Müller tube and ratemeter, measure the background level

A3 Since the (corrected) activity falls from 80 Bq to 20 Bq in 40 days, it follows that two half-lives have passed in this time, giving a half-life of 20 days

examiner's note Other precautions include minimising the length of time needed to carry out the work and using a lead castle to direct rays in one direction only. You must use background-corrected data in all calculations.

Experiments with radioactivity II

Q1 How would you distinguish between alpha, beta and gamma rays?

Q2 What method would you use to measure the half-life of a radioisotope with (a) a short half-life and (b) a long half-life?

Q3 Why do alpha and beta rays not obey the inverse square law (as gamma rays do)?

ANSWERS

A1 Insert thin paper between the source and the Geiger–Müller tube. If a large drop in count rate occurs, alpha rays are present. Then place a 5 mm thick aluminium sheet in the beam. If a large drop in count rate is observed (or it falls to zero), then beta rays are present. If the activity is still well above background, then gamma rays are being emitted.

A2 (a) Measure the (background-corrected) activity and plot this against time. Half-life is found by measuring the time taken for the activity to fall to half its original value. (b) Find the mass of the sample, divide by the atomic mass of the element and then proceed as in question 3, Topic 30

A3 Since alpha and beta particles are highly ionising, energy is lost by ionising air molecules between the source and the Geiger–Müller tube

***examiner's* note** Alternative methods to distinguish between the three types of ray include the use of electric or magnetic fields in the path of the beam in an attempt to deflect them and the use of a Geiger–Müller tube and ratemeter.

Scattering experiments

Q1 What is (a) the target and (b) the particle used in the Rutherford back scattering experiment? (c) What three deductions may be drawn from this experiment?

Q2 What is (a) the target and (b) the particle used in the deep inelastic scattering experiment?

Q3 What particle(s) were discovered as a result of the deep inelastic scattering experiment?

ANSWERS

A1 (a) Thin gold foil

(b) Alpha particle

(c) The atom consists of mainly empty space; nuclei are positively charged; nuclei are incredibly small compared to overall atomic size

A2 (a) Liquid hydrogen (or protons)

(b) High-energy electrons

A3 Quarks were discovered

***examiner's* note** In the deep inelastic scattering experiment, if atoms were homogeneous, electrons would suffer no deviation.

Exchange particles

Complete the following table:

Force	Acts on	Exchange particle	Symbol
gravity			
electromagnetic			
nuclear (weak)			
nuclear (strong)			

ANSWERS))

Force	Acts on	Exchange particle	Symbol
gravity	particles with mass	graviton	G
electromagnetic	particles with charge	photon	γ
nuclear (weak)	all particles	intermediate vector bosons	W^+, W^-, Z^0
nuclear (strong)	quarks and hadrons	gluons	g

***examiner's* note** Gravitons and gluons remain hypothetical. Photons are particles of electromagnetic radiation.

Nuclear forces

Q1 Name six quantities that must be conserved in any interaction.

Q2 Name the forces that could act between the following particles:
(a) two electrons, (b) an electron and a neutron,
(c) a proton and a neutron and (d) a quark and an antiquark.

Q3 A neutron-rich radionuclide may decay by β^- emission; a
neutron is converted into a proton. (a) Write an equation for
this process. (b) Which force is involved in this process?
(c) Which exchange particle is involved?

ANSWERS

A1 Mass–energy, charge, momentum, baryon number, lepton number and strangeness

A2 (a) Electromagnetic and weak interaction
   (b) Weak interaction
   (c) Strong interaction and weak interaction
   (d) Strong interaction and weak interaction

A3 (a) $_0^1n = {}_1^1p + {}_{-1}^0e + \bar{\nu}_e$
   (b) Weak nuclear force
   (c) W^-

examiner's note Mass and energy are now considered as one entity: mass–energy.

Composition of particles

Q1 Give the composition, charge and baryon number for
(a) a neutron and (b) a proton.

Q2 (a) What type of particle is a pion (pi meson)?
(b) Pions also consist of u and d quarks and antiquarks. Give the
composition, charge and baryon number for π^+, π^-, π^0.

Q3 A pion can decay into a muon. What type of particle is a muon?

ANSWERS

A1 (a) Neutron: ddu, charge = 0, B = 1
   (b) Proton: uud, charge = +1, B = 1

A2 (a) A pion is a hadron
   (b) π^+: $u\bar{d}$, charge = +1; B = 0; π^-: $d\bar{u}$, charge = −1, B = 0;
   π^0: $u\bar{u}$ or $d\bar{d}$, charge = 0, B = 0

A3 A muon is a lepton

***examiner's* note** Up quarks (u) have a charge of +2/3; down quarks (d) have a charge of −1/3. Both have baryon numbers of 1/3.

Particles and anti-particles

Q1 What are the three characteristics relating particles to antiparticles?

Q2 What is the antiparticle of (a) the electron, (b) the proton and (c) the neutrino?

Q3 State two differences (a) between leptons and hadrons and (b) between mesons and baryons.

ANSWERS

A1 • A particle and its antiparticle have equal and opposite charge
   • A particle has the same mass as its antiparticle
   • An unstable particle and its antiparticle have the same lifetime

A2 (a) The positron
   (b) The antiproton
   (c) The antineutrino

A3 (a) Leptons are fundamental particles; hadrons are not
   fundamental particles. Hadrons are particles that can take part in
   strong interactions; leptons cannot.
   (b) All mesons are unstable; all baryons, except the proton, are
   unstable. All baryons are fermions; all mesons are bosons.

examiner's note Each type of particle has an antiparticle. Antiparticles are not
constituents of ordinary matter. They can be created when cosmic rays interact
with matter, as a result of radioactive decay or when particles collide in high-
energy accelerators.

Conservation laws in particle physics

Q1 Although strangeness is conserved in all strong and all electromagnetic interactions, how does it change in weak interactions?

Q2 Which of these reactions is not allowed?
(a) $\pi^+ + p \rightarrow K^+ + n$ (c) $p + p \rightarrow p + p + \pi^0$
(b) $K^+ + \bar{p} \rightarrow \pi^0$

Q3 Use conservation laws for charge, baryon number and strangeness and data tables to identify particle X:
(a) $K^- + p \rightarrow K^+ + K^0 + X$ (c) $K^0 + p \rightarrow K^+ + X$
(b) $\pi^+ + n \rightarrow \Lambda^0 + X$

ANSWERS

A1 In weak interactions, it changes by ±1 or 0.

A2 (a) Not allowed (b) Not allowed (c) Allowed

A3 (a) Ω^- (b) K^+ (c) n

***examiner's* note** In question 2, reaction (a) contravenes charge conservation and strangeness conservation. Reaction (b) contravenes baryon number and strangeness conservation.

Feynman diagrams

Q1 What are the simple rules for writing and interpreting Feynman diagrams?

Q2 Draw the Feynman diagrams for (a) electron–electron scattering and (b) positron emission in which a proton transforms into a neutron, emitting a positron and electron neutrino.

ANSWERS ▶▶

A1 Incident particles move up the diagram from the bottom. A W boson transfers charge between particles and is shown as a wavy line; left-to-right represents time; up-and-down represents particle motion — without any attempt to show direction or speed.

A2 (a)

(b)

***examiner's* note** In question 2(a) electric repulsion between two electrons might be explained as one electron emits a photon and recoils, the second electron absorbs the photon and acquires its momentum.

Electric charge

Q1 What is (a) the SI unit and (b) the base unit for charge?

Q2 What is the relationship between current, charge and time?

Q3 What significant physical feature is there about electric charge?

ANSWERS

A1 (a) coulomb (C)
(b) $1\,C = 1\,A\,s$

A2 charge = current × time

A3 It is quantised, i.e. it is discrete or comes in distinct packets

examiner's note The coulomb is defined as the charge passing any given point when 1 amp flows for 1 second. Millikan, experimenting with falling charged oil drops in electric fields, discovered the value of e in 1909.

Conduction in solids, liquids and gases

Q1 What is the physical significance of the area under a current–time graph?

Q2 What is the physical significance of the gradient of the charge–time graph?

Q3 How do (a) metals, (b) electrolytes and (c) gases at low pressure conduct electricity?

ANSWERS

A1 The total electric charge passed during the time in question

A2 The current, or rate of flow of charge ($I = dQ/dt$)

A3 (a) By the flow of free electrons
   (b) By the motion of ions, when molten or in aqueous solution
   (c) By the motion of gaseous ions

examiner's note Measuring the area under a current–time graph is especially useful in experiments involving the charging (or discharging) of capacitors. Metals possess a large number of free electrons that move under the influence of a potential difference. Solid electrolytes are not electrical conductors since their ions are not mobile.

Ohm's law and *I–V* curves

Q1 (a) State Ohm's law. (b) Define electrical resistance.

Q2 Give (a) the SI unit and (b) the base unit of electrical resistance.

Q3 How can the resistance of a component be found from its *I–V* characteristics?

ANSWERS ⟩⟩

A1 (a) The current flowing through a conductor is proportional to the potential difference across its ends, provided that temperature remains constant

(b) Opposition to the flow of current

A2 (a) the ohm (Ω)

(b) kg m^2 s^{-3} A^{-2}

A3 The resistance of a component is the value of V/I, or the gradient of a voltage–current graph, where V is the y-axis and I is the x-axis

examiner's **note** The base unit may be found using $R = V/I$. 1 volt = 1 joule per coulomb = N m/A s, then use $F = ma$ to work out the base unit for N. A more precise value for resistance is obtained from the I–V characteristics since the best straight line is drawn and any deviations from constant resistance are readily found.

Drift velocity of electrons

Q1 How is current related to the drift velocity of charge carriers?

Q2 Explain why, although the drift velocity of electrons in a copper wire is very slow, your electric lamp comes on at almost the same instant as you close the switch.

Q3 A slab of metal is joined to a slab of semiconductor of the same cross-sectional area and a current is passed through the assembly, so that they are in series. Compare the values of *n* and *v* in each material.

ANSWERS

A1 $I = nAvq$, where I = current (A); n = carrier concentration (m^{-3}); A = cross-sectional area (m^2); v = drift velocity of charge carriers ($m\,s^{-1}$); q = charge on particle (C)

A2 The signal that starts the electrons moving travels at the speed of light. It is not necessary for an electron that was originally next to the switch to light the lamp.

A3 Slabs are in series, so current through metal equals current through semiconductor. A and q are common to both. Since n is very high for metals and v is small, it follows that because n is much lower for semiconductors, then the drift velocity in semiconductors is much higher.

***examiner's* note** The problem in question 3 could also be solved mathematically, using the relationship $I = n_1Av_1q = n_2Av_2q$.

Metals, semiconductors and insulators I

Q1 What is the difference between a metal and a semiconductor?

Q2 What is the effect of temperature on the resistance of semiconductors?

Q3 What is the effect of temperature on the resistance of metals?

ANSWERS

A1 Metals have large numbers of free electrons; semiconductors have far fewer free electrons

A2 An increase in temperature reduces the resistance of a semiconductor

A3 An increase in temperature increases the resistance of a metal

examiner's note Metals have full conduction bands of free electrons, whereas those in semiconductors are only partially filled (and are empty at 0 K).

Metals, semiconductors and insulators II

Q1 What is an electrical insulator? Classify the following as metal, semiconductor or insulator: (a) glass, (b) iron, (c) silicon, (d) paraffin wax, (e) graphite, (f) copper and (g) porcelain.

Q2 Explain the effect of temperature on the resistance of semiconductors.

Q3 Explain the effect of temperature on the resistance of metals.

ANSWERS

A1 In an insulator, the valence band energy levels are completely filled with electrons. The conduction band is empty and the two bands are separated by a large energy gap.
   (a) Insulator (b) Metal (c) Semiconductor (d) Insulator
   (e) Semiconductor (f) Metal (g) Insulator

A2 An increase in temperature increases the energy of the electrons, which means that some of them are able to 'jump' the energy gap between the valence and conduction bands, thereby increasing the value of n (number of electrons joining in the conduction process)

A3 Increased vibration of the ion cores impedes the motion of electrons through the metallic lattice, thereby reducing their drift speed

examiner's note In metals, the valence and conduction bands can overlap; in semiconductors, however, there is a 'band gap' between valence and conduction bands, which electrons cannot occupy. In insulators, the band gap is very large.

Resistivity

Q1 Explain what is meant by resistivity. What is its SI unit?

Q2 Give two precautions to be taken in the measurement of resistivity in order to maximise precision.

Q3 If the cross-sectional area of the live rail of an electric railway is $50\,cm^2$ and the resistivity of steel is $1.0 \times 10^{-7}\,\Omega\,m$, calculate the resistance per kilometre, neglecting the effect of joints.

ANSWERS

A1 $\text{resistance} = \dfrac{\text{resistivity} \times \text{length}}{\text{cross-sectional area}}$. SI unit: $\Omega\,\text{m}$.

A2 Keep the current low to avoid overheating the wire; when taking measurements, minimise the time of current flow

A3 $R = \dfrac{\rho L}{A} = \dfrac{1.0 \times 10^{-7} \times 1.0 \times 10^{3}}{50 \times 10^{-4}} = 2.0 \times 10^{-2}\,\Omega$

examiner's note Other possible precautions include measuring the diameter of the wire at several points and averaging, using high-precision digital ammeters and voltmeters and avoiding kinks in the wire.

Effect of temperature and light on resistance

Q1 (a) What is a light-dependent resistor (LDR)?

(b) How does its resistance vary with illumination?

Q2 Give two applications where LDRs are used.

Q3 (a) What is an NTC thermistor?

(b) Give two applications where thermistors are used.

ANSWERS ▶▶

A1 (a) A semiconductor device whose resistance varies with Illumination (b) The resistance falls from a high value in the dark to a low value in bright light

A2 Switching circuits for street lighting and exposure meters for cameras

A3 (a) A thermistor is a heat-sensitive resistor, made from semiconductors. In the case of a negative temperature coefficient (NTC) thermistor, its resistance falls when its temperature is increased. (b) To safeguard against current surges where components may be damaged and in resistance thermometers for the measurement of very low temperatures

***examiner's* note** Some thermistors have a high positive temperature coefficient (PTC) of resistance. When a PTC thermistor is placed in series with a cell and warmed, the current falls because of increased resistance. There may be applications in which this type of behaviour is desirable, e.g. a high-temperature, platinum-wound resistance furnace which might be damaged by high initial currents.

 **ANSWERS**

Electrical power

Q1 Give three equations for electrical power.

Q2 Compare the power dissipation in two resistors (one small and one large) (a) in series and (b) in parallel.

Q3 The voltage of a mains circuit is 230 V and the fuse rating is 13 A. How many 0.5 kW devices can be connected across the circuit before the fuse blows?

ANSWERS

A1 power, $P = IV = I^2R = V^2/R$

A2 (a) Since the current is common to both resistors, it follows
    that greater power is dissipated in the larger resistor, using the
    equation $P = I^2R$ (b) Since the potential difference is common to
    both resistors, it follows that more power is dissipated in the
    smaller resistor, since $P = V^2/R$

A3 Current flowing through each device, $I = P/V = 500/230 = 2.17\,A$.
    Since the current that can be drawn from the mains is 13 A, then
    if there are n devices, then $2.17 \times n = 13$. So, $n = 13/2.7 = 4.81$,
    giving $n = 4$.

***examiner's* note** Since energy = power × time, it follows that electrical energy
supplied (in joules) is equal to any of the the three expressions above multiplied
by time (seconds). Other equations for power may be used in question 2. In
question 3, the devices are connected in parallel. For safety, the result is 'rounded
down'.

Kirchhoff's first and second laws

Q1 State Kirchhoff's first law.

Q2 State Kirchhoff's second law.

Q3 What electrical quantity is conserved in (a) Kirchhoff's first law and (b) Kirchhoff's second law?

ANSWERS

A1 The algebraic sum of the currents at a junction is zero

A2 Around any closed loop, the sum of the emfs is equal to the sum of the potential differences

A3 (a) Charge
(b) Energy

***examiner's* note** Kirchhoff extended Ohm's law to networks (complicated systems of electrical conductors) by formulating two laws. Taken together, these laws mean that you can calculate the current at any point in a network.

Ohm's law for a complete circuit

Q1 What is Ohm's law for a complete circuit?

Q2 What graph is plotted to find the emf of a battery and its internal resistance, and how are they found from the graph?

Q3 What is the 'maximum power' theorem?

ANSWERS

A1 $E/I = (R + r)$, where E = emf of cell; r = internal resistance of cell

A2 Plot the terminal potential difference on the y-axis and the current on the x-axis. The intercept on the y-axis is the emf of the cell. The gradient (negative) of the straight-line graph is the internal resistance of the cell.

A3 The maximum power delivered by a cell occurs when $R = r$

***examiner's* note** The internal resistance of a cell actually occurs inside it, between the positive and negative terminals, but in a circuit diagram it is drawn outside the cell (for simplicity). The equation used for the graph may be rewritten as $V = E - Ir$, where V = terminal potential difference. Note in question 3 that this is maximum power, not maximum current.

Internal resistance I

Q1 What resistance should (a) a car battery and (b) a 5 kV high-voltage power supply have?

Q2 What problems may arise when low internal resistance batteries, such as rechargeable nickel–cadmium batteries, are accidentally short-circuited?

Q3 Estimate the internal resistance of a new 1.5 V AA battery.

ANSWERS

A1 (a) Very low (e.g. $0.01\,\Omega$)

(b) Very high (e.g. $10\,M\Omega$)

A2 Overheating, leading to burns or a fire being started

A3 Ohm's law gives $r = E/I = 1.5/3.0 = 0.5\,\Omega$, since the battery typically provides 3 A on short circuit

***examiner's* note** A car battery needs to have a small internal resistance since it needs to supply very high currents. Power supplies over 5 kV can supply lethally high currents if you touch them accidentally. So, to prevent this, very high internal resistances need to be used to ensure that the currents are only small. Accidents have occurred involving metal keys in the same pocket as nickel–cadmium batteries. The large, short-circuit current heats up the keys, causing burns.

Internal resistance II

Q1 A high-resistance voltmeter reads 6.2 V when placed across the terminals of a battery. If the battery is now connected to a 15 Ω resistor, the reading changes to 6.0 V. Calculate (a) the emf of the cell and (b) its internal resistance.

Q2 A fully charged car battery has an emf of 14.2 V. If it drives a current of 220 A through a resistance of 0.06 Ω, calculate the internal resistance of the battery.

Q3 After the battery in question 2 has been used for some time, it has a resistance of 0.2 Ω. Calculate the current that flows when connected to the same circuit.

ANSWERS

A1 (a) By definition, emf of battery = 6.2 V (b) pd across internal resistance = emf − pd across external resistance = 6.2 − 6.0 = 0.2 V. Current through circuit, $I = V/R = 6.0/15 = 0.4$ A. Since this is a series circuit, 0.4 A also flows through r, giving $r = 0.2/0.4 = 0.5\ \Omega$.

A2 pd across internal resistance = $E − IR = 14.2 − (220 \times 0.06) = 1.0$ V. Since this is also a series arrangement, 220 A also flows through r, giving $r = 1.0/220 = 0.0045\ \Omega$.

A3 $I = E/(R + r) = 14.2/(0.06 + 0.2) = 14.2/0.26 = 54.6$ A

***examiner's* note:** Question 2: car batteries have a nominal emf of 12 V. In reality, it is usually greater than this. Note the low internal resistance and the high current passed through a low external resistance. Question 3: in old or discharged batteries, a greatly reduced current passes through the (same) external resistor.

Resistors in series and parallel I

Q1 What is the general formula for three resistors (a) in series and (b) in parallel?

Q2 Three $10\,\Omega$ resistors may be connected together in four different ways. Describe these ways and calculate the resistance in each case.

Q3 For ammeters and voltmeters, describe (a) their ideal resistances and (b) their correct connections to components in a circuit.

ANSWERS

A1 (a) $R = R_1 + R_2 + R_3$ (b) $1/R = 1/R_1 + 1/R_2 + 1/R_3$

A2 • All in series: $R = 10 + 10 + 10 = 30\,\Omega$
- All in parallel: $1/R = 1/10 + 1/10 + 1/10 = 3/10$; giving $R = 3.3\,\Omega$
- Two in parallel and one in series: $1/R = 1/10 + 1/10 = 2/10$, giving $R = 5\,\Omega$ for parallel loop; total resistance $= 10 + 5 = 15\,\Omega$
- Two resistors in series ($20\,\Omega$) in parallel with one resistor: $1/R = 1/20 + 1/10 = 3/20$, giving $R = 6.7\,\Omega$

A3 (a) Ideal resistance of ammeters is zero and of voltmeters is infinite
(b) Ammeters are placed in series and voltmeters are placed in parallel

***examiner's* note** You should be able to prove the relationships in answer 1, if asked to do so in an examination. In question 2, two other arrangements are also possible: 'star formation', in which one end of each resistor is joined to the others and where the resistance between any two ends is $20\,\Omega$ ($10\,\Omega + 10\,\Omega$), and a 'delta formation', where the resistance across any two ends is the same as the final option given above.

Resistors in series and parallel II

Q1 Four identical lamps are placed in a simple DC circuit such that one lamp (A) is in series with the remaining three (B, C and D) in parallel. If all are lit and one lamp is then removed from the parallel loop, describe how the brightness of the lamps changes.

Q2 Four $20\,\Omega$ resistors are connected such that two of them are placed in series and placed in parallel with the remaining two resistors, also in series. Calculate the total resistance of the network.

Q3 If a current flows through three wires of $5\,\Omega$, $10\,\Omega$ and $20\,\Omega$ in parallel, how is the current shared in each resistor?

ANSWERS

A1 First, lamp A will be brighter than the (equally bright) lamps B, C and D. When one lamp is removed from the parallel arrangement, all lamps will be dimmer than originally, but A will still be brighter than those in the loop.

A2 Total resistance of parallel network, $1/R = 1/40 + 1/40 = 1/20$, giving $R = 20\,\Omega$. This combination may be used to replace a single $20\,\Omega$ resistor, since the heating effect is less than in any single resistor, because a smaller current flows through each resistor.

A3 The current is shared in the ratio $1/5 : 1/10 : 1/20$ or $4:2:1$

***examiner's* note** In question 1, the resistance of the parallel network will increase when one lamp is removed, thus increasing the total circuit resistance — which explains the overall dimming of the lamps. A will be brighter since all the current in the 'main' circuit flows through it. In question 3, currents in parallel networks divide in inverse proportion to their resistances.

Potential dividers

Q1 What is meant by a potential divider?

Q2 Two lamps, one rated 240 V/60 W; the other, 3 V/0.75 W are connected in series with the 240 V mains supply. If both lamps are lit normally, calculate the potential difference across each lamp.

Q3 Give two applications in which sensors may be used as part of potential dividers.

ANSWERS

A1 Two resistors in series, used to provide a known fraction of a given potential difference.

A2 When operating normally, each lamp draws a current of 0.25 A. This gives resistances of $240/0.25 = 960\,\Omega$ and $3/0.25 = 12\,\Omega$ respectively. Thus, the potential difference across the mains lamp $= 960/(960 + 12) \times 240 = 237\,V$. Similarly, the potential difference across the low-voltage lamp $= 12/(960 + 12) \times 240 = 2.96\,V$.

A3 Light and temperature sensors may be incorporated into potential dividers to vary output voltages, depending upon ambient conditions. The light sensor (LDR) has a low resistance in bright light, and a high resistance in darkness. Temperature sensors have low resistances when hot, and a high resistance when cold.

***examiner's* note** We may calculate the output voltage, V_{out}, from the input voltage, V_{in}. If the resistors involved are R_1 and R_2, then V_{out} (across R_1) $= V_{in} \times R_1/(R_1 + R_2)$. Remember, for this equation to hold, it is assumed that no current is drawn from R_2.

DC circuit theory I

Q1 Define electromotive force (emf) of a cell or battery.

Q2 Express voltage in base units.

Q3 2000 W of power is to be transmitted through a cable of resistance 2 Ω. Compare the power losses by using (a) a current of 10 A at 200 V and (b) a current of 1 A at 2000 V. Comment on your answer.

ANSWERS

A1 The emf of a cell, battery or other power source is the total energy per coulomb that it delivers round a circuit connected to it

A2 $kg\,m^2\,s^{-3}\,A^{-1}$

A3 (a) Power dissipated = $I^2R = (10)^2 \times 2 = 200$ W, which is 10% of the power fed into the cable

(b) $I^2R = (1)^2 \times 2 = 2$ W, which is only 0.1% of the power fed into the cable

***examiner's* note** Since $P = IV$, it follows that $V = P/I =$ Nm/As, from which we may readily obtain the answer. Alternatively, 1 volt = 1 joule per coulomb, which gives the same result. The calculations in answer 3 show that transmitting power at an increased voltage gives a greatly reduced power loss.

DC circuit theory II

Q1 A battery of negligible internal resistance delivers $200\,\mu A$ to a $25\,k\Omega$ resistor. What is the emf of the battery?

Q2 A voltmeter is then connected across the resistor, and the milliammeter now reads $250\,\mu A$. Calculate the resistance of the voltmeter.

Q3 Calculate the heat produced in a $10\,\Omega$ resistor when a current of $2.0\,A$ flows through it for 1 minute.

ANSWERS

A1 Ohm's law gives $E = IR = 200 \times 10^{-6} \times 25 \times 10^3 = 5.00$ V

A2 New total resistance of circuit is $R = E/I = 5.00/(250 \times 10^{-6}) = 20\,k\Omega$.

Let the resistance of the voltmeter be R_v, then for resistors in parallel: $1/R_{tot} = 1/R + 1/R_v$, or $1/20 = 1/25 + 1/R_v$, giving $R_v = 100\,k\Omega$.

A3 Electrical energy supplied $= I^2Rt = (2.0)^2 \times 10 \times 1 \times 60 = 2400$ J

examiner's note Question 2 shows the effect of voltmeters having a finite resistance. If the voltmeter had infinite resistance, there would be no change in the milliammeter reading. Note that this calculation has been carried out in units of $k\Omega$. Energy = power × time = $I^2R \times t$. Take care in questions involving time — you need to convert from minutes to seconds.

AC circuit theory I

Q1 Define the terms 'time period' and 'frequency' for an alternating current.

Q2 Define the rms voltage of an alternating sinusoidal signal in terms of the peak voltage.

Q3 Why are rms values for current and voltage used to calculate the power of an AC supply rather than the peak values?

ANSWERS

A1 The time period is the time between successive peaks of voltage (or current); frequency = 1/time period

A2 $V_{rms} = V_0/\sqrt{2}$, where V_{rms} = root-mean-square voltage and V_0 = peak voltage

A3 It works out that the power of an AC supply = $I_{rms} \times V_{rms}$

examiner's note In question 2 it also follows that the root-mean-square current, $I_{rms} = I_0/\sqrt{2}$, where I_0 is the peak current. In question 3, the root-mean-square value of an alternating current is defined as the value of steady current that would dissipate heat at the same rate in a given resistance.

AC circuit theory II

Q1 The rms value of a sinusoidal alternating current is 2.0 A. What is (a) its peak value; (b) the peak value of the pd across a 12 Ω resistor and (c) the power dissipation in the resistor?

Q2 For a sinusoidal alternating current, $I = 18 \sin (100\pi t)$, what is (a) the peak value of the current; (b) the rms current; (c) the supply frequency and (d) the time period of the supply?

Q3 A square-wave alternating pd is as follows: for 1.0 ms the pd is constant at its peak value $+V_0$. The pd changes rapidly to the value $-V_0$, where it remains for a further 1.0 ms. It reverts equally rapidly to the initial value $+V_0$ etc. What are the rms value and the half-cycle average value of this alternating pd?

 ANSWERS

A1 (a) $2.0 \times \sqrt{2} = 2.8$ A (b) $V = I \times R = 2.8 \times 12 = 33.6$ V

(c) $P = I_{rms} \times V_{rms} = 2.0 \times 33.6/\sqrt{2} = 48$ W

A2 (a) $I_0 = 18$ A (b) $I_{rms} = 18/\sqrt{2} = 12.7$ A (c) $50\,Hz$ (d) $0.02\,s$

A3 Both values $= V_0$

examiner's note In question 2 the equation is of the type $I = I_0 \sin(2\pi ft)$, where I = current at time t, I_0 = peak current, f = frequency, $T = 1/f$. In question 3, sketching a graph of this waveform helps you find its solution.

Hooke's law and spring constant

Q1 State Hooke's law and explain the 'elastic limit'.

Q2 Define the spring constant (k) and give its SI unit.

Q3 How may the spring constant be found experimentally?

ANSWERS

A1 Extension is directly proportional to the applied load (force) for a wire or spring, provided that the elastic limit is not exceeded. Beyond the elastic limit, permanent deformation occurs.

A2 The force per unit extension of the spring.
Since $F = kx$, its SI unit is Nm^{-1}.

A3 If a plot of load (y-axis) against extension (x-axis) is made, then the gradient = k

***examiner's* note** To check that the elastic limit has not been exceeded, the specimen should be loaded and unloaded, and you should get the same results from both parts of the experiment. The spring constant may also be found by timing oscillations with a known mass.

Stress–strain curves and Young's modulus I

Q1 Define (a) stress, (b) strain and (c) Young's modulus (*E*). Give their SI units.

Q2 Why are long, thin wires used in the experimental measurement of *E*?

Q3 Why are two similar wires used in the experiment to determine *E*?

ANSWERS 》

A1 (a) Force per unit area (N m^{-2} or Pa) (b) Change in length per unit length (dimensionless) (c) Stress/strain (N m^{-2} or Pa)

A2 Long wires are used in order to obtain as large an extension as possible. Thin wires are used in order to get a high stress without the need for heavy weights.

A3 When the test wire is loaded, there is a tendency for its support to sag. Errors associated with this may be avoided by carrying the reference scale on a second wire suspended from the same beam. Both wires are made from the same material and are of the same length to avoid errors due to expansion as a result of temperature changes during the experiment.

***examiner's* note** Wires used are typically 2 m long, their diameters being about 1 mm maximum. A Vernier arrangement allows precise measurements of extensions.

Stress–strain curves and Young's modulus II

Q1 How may (a) Young's modulus and (b) ultimate tensile strength (UTS) be found from stress–strain curves?

Q2 Describe the stress–strain curves of (a) glass, (b) rubber and (c) copper.

Q3 What is the 'yield point'?

ANSWERS ▶▶

A1 (a) Young's modulus = gradient of linear portion of stress–strain curve (b) UTS = maximum value of stress reached on the curve

A2 (a) Nearly all elastic behaviour (straight line), fracturing at very low strain with virtually no plastic flow (b) A curve, with no linear portion, giving very high strains for low stresses. On removing the stress, the curve follows a different path downwards (hysteresis). (c) A linear region initially, up to a small strain, followed by a large 'dome-shaped' region at moderate strains, until the stress falls and the material fractures

A3 The point at which there is a marked increase in extension if stress is increased beyond the elastic limit. The material then shows plastic behaviour.

***examiner's* note** Young's modulus is a measure of the stiffness of a material. UTS, or the 'tensile strength', is a measure of the strength of a specimen. Only a few materials show yielding, mild steel being the best known.

Work done in stretching wires

Q1 What is the work done in stretching a wire?

Q2 What is the work done per unit volume in stretching a wire?

Q3 A steel bar has a rectangular cross-section 50 mm by 40 mm and is 2.0 m long. Calculate the work done in extending it by 6.0 mm. Take E for steel as $2.0 \times 10^{11}\,\mathrm{N\,m^{-2}}$.

ANSWERS ▶▶

A1 Work done in stretching a wire, $W = \frac{1}{2} \times$ force $\times$ extension = $\frac{1}{2}Fe$

A2 Work done per unit volume = $\frac{1}{2} \times$ stress $\times$ strain = $\frac{1}{2}\sigma\varepsilon$

A3 Work done per unit volume = $\frac{1}{2}E\varepsilon^2 = \frac{1}{2} \times 2 \times 10^{11} \times (6/2000)^2 = 9.0 \times 10^5\,J$

Volume = $2.0 \times 50 \times 40 \times 10^{-6} = 4 \times 10^{-3}\,m^3$, so work done = $3.6\,kJ$

***examiner's* note** Energy/volume = $\frac{1}{2}\sigma\varepsilon = (\frac{1}{2})(\sigma/\varepsilon) \times \varepsilon^2 = \frac{1}{2}E\varepsilon^2$. Similarly, work done in stretching a wire = $\frac{1}{2}ke^2$, where k is the spring constant and e the extension.

Ductility and brittleness

Q1 Define (a) ductility, (b) brittleness and (c) toughness.

Q2 What is meant by (a) elastic deformation and (b) plastic deformation? How are these related to ductility and brittleness?

Q3 What is the ductile/brittle transition temperature and how is it measured?

ANSWERS

A1 (a) A ductile material can be stretched easily and permanently
(b) A brittle material cannot be stretched permanently; when a tensile force is applied, the material breaks soon after the elastic limit has been reached
(c) In a tough material, a large amount of work is needed to break it

A2 (a) The specimen returns to its original length after the stress is removed (b) Permanent deformation remains, even after the removal of stress. All the deformation in ductile materials is plastic; most of the deformation in brittle materials is elastic.

A3 This is the temperature at which the fracture surface appears 50% ductile:50% brittle. It is found by impact loading over a wide range of temperatures and examining the fracture surfaces.

***examiner's* note** Only certain materials show ductile/brittle transition temperature behaviour. For example, aluminium is ductile at all temperatures.

Structure of materials

Q1 What is meant by (a) an amorphous material, (b) a crystalline material, (c) a polycrystalline material, (d) a polymer and (e) a single crystal?

Q2 Give one example of each type of material in question 1.

Q3 Give examples of (a) two ductile metals and (b) brittle materials (one metal and one non-metal).

ANSWERS ▶▶

A1 (a) A material whose particles have no long-range order
(b) A material consisting of particles in a regular lattice
(c) A material consisting of grains in which the atom planes are all aligned in the same direction; however, grains have different directions (d) Polymers are made chemically from monomers and contain long chains of carbon (or silicon) atoms, joined to hydrogen or other atoms (e) In a single crystal, order extends right through the solid

A2 (a) Glass (b) Ionic solid (any) (c) Any commercially available metal or alloy (d) Polythene (e) A silicon single crystal

A3 (a) Copper, aluminium (b) Cast iron, glass

***examiner's* note** Metals may be 'glassy' or amorphous if rapidly quenched from the liquid state, e.g. at a rate of $10^6 \,°C\,s^{-1}$. The random structure of the liquid is then 'frozen' in the solid. Samples of single crystal silicon and germanium are used in semiconductor devices.

 65 ANSWERS

Work hardening and annealing

Q1 What is cold work?

Q2 What is annealing?

Q3 How may cold work and annealing be used to improve the properties of a metal?

ANSWERS

A1 A process in which the crystal structure is plastically deformed, giving the material a higher strength and hardness, but lower ductility and toughness (an increase in brittleness). It may be carried out by cold-rolling, wire-drawing or stretching the specimen.

A2 Annealing involves heating a metal to a high temperature (but below its melting point) for a length of time, followed by slow cooling

A3 The cold work/anneal cycle is commonly used to improve the room-temperature mechanical properties (e.g. strength) of metals and alloys by reducing the grain size

examiner's note Cold work is accompanied by an increase in dislocation density and their pinning or locking/intersecting with each other.

Polymer and rubber properties

Q1 What is meant by hysteresis in rubber?

Q2 What sort of rubber should be used (a) to make car tyres and (b) for buffers in dodgem cars?

Q3 Distinguish between thermosets and thermoplastic polymers.

ANSWERS 》

A1 On loading and unloading a sample of rubber with tensile forces, the stress–strain curve does not follow the same path; there may be a small permanent elongation when the load is removed (called a 'permanent set')

A2 (a) A resilient one — i.e. one that has a small hysteresis loop in order to minimise heating the tyre (b) One with a large hysteresis loop, so as to absorb large amounts of energy

A3 A thermoset is a polymer that forms a network, with cross-links between chains (like a fishnet). However, thermoplastics may be readily moulded or extruded because of the absence of cross-links. A thermo-plastic becomes plastic if the temperature is raised and can be remoulded into shape, even at temperatures below the melting point.

***examiner's* note** Impacts between dodgems are infrequent and masses so large that significant temperature rises are unlikely, which differs from the case of car tyres.

Composite materials

Q1 What is a composite material?

Q2 What are the three classes of composite material? Give one example of each used or seen in everyday life.

Q3 Describe how a pre-stressed reinforced concrete beam is produced.

ANSWERS))

A1 A composite material is one in which two materials are combined in order to use the properties of both.

A2 Particle, e.g. chipboard; laminate, e.g. plywood; fibre, e.g. fibreglass

A3 Concrete has many favourable features, e.g. it can be cast into any shape, it is cheap and it is fire-resistant. Although it has a low tensile strength and low ductility, its performance is improved if allowed to set around steel wire. The steel wire hinders the formation of cracks through the concrete. Even greater strengthening may be obtained if the concrete is put into compression, by applying a tensile force to the steel, while allowing the concrete to set around the steel.

examiner's **note** A drawback with composites is that, because of the sophisticated techniques required to make them, they are expensive and so the number of applications remains fairly constant.

Wave motion I

Q1 Define wave motion.

Q2 Give four general properties of waves.

Q3 Distinguish between longitudinal and transverse waves.

ANSWERS ▶▶

A1 A means of transferring energy from one point to another without any matter being transferred

A2 Reflection, refraction, diffraction and interference

A3 In a transverse wave, the disturbed particles vibrate at 90° to the direction of travel of the wave. In a longitudinal wave, particles vibrate in the direction of travel of the wave.

***examiner's* note** An example from everyday experience is light and heat travelling from the Sun to the Earth through the vacuum of space (as no matter is transported).

Wave motion II

Q1 Classify the following types of wave: (a) sound waves, (b) surface waves on water, (c) waves on a string, (d) electromagnetic waves and (e) sound waves sounding organ pipes.

Q2 Explain what is meant by (a) the amplitude, (b) the frequency and (c) the wavelength of a wave.

Q3 (a) Give the general equation for wave motion. (b) In the equation $x = 0.025 \sin(500\pi t)$, what is the value of the amplitude and the frequency of the wave?

ANSWERS

A1 (a) Sound waves are longitudinal (b) Surface waves are transverse (c) Waves on a string are transverse (d) Electromagnetic waves are transverse (e) Sound waves in sounding organ pipes are longitudinal

A2 (a) The amplitude is the maximum displacement of the wave from its rest position (b) The frequency of the wave is the number of crests or troughs passing a fixed point in 1 second
(c) The wavelength is the distance between two adjacent crests or the distance between two particles vibrating in phase

A3 (a) $x = x_0 \sin(2\pi ft)$, where x = displacement after any time t, f is the frequency of the wave and x_0 is the amplitude of the wave
(b) Amplitude = 0.025 m, frequency is given by $2\pi f = 500\pi$, i.e. frequency = 250 Hz

examiner's **note** Give exact definitions in question 2 as vague answers will not score marks.

Wave speed

Q1 How are the velocity, frequency and wavelength of a wave related?

Q2 The velocity v of ocean waves in terms of g, the acceleration of free fall, and the wavelength λ is given by $v = \sqrt{g\lambda}$. Show that this equation is dimensionally homogeneous with respect to units.

Q3 A passing ship generates plane waves that take 150 s to reach a floating buoy 60 m away. The buoy subsequently oscillates with simple harmonic motion with a period of 9.0 s. Determine the wavelength of the waves.

ANSWERS

A1 wave velocity = frequency × wavelength; $c = f \times \lambda$

A2 v has units of ms^{-1}, so the right-hand side of the equation should have the same units. g has units of ms^{-2}, λ has units of m. $\sqrt{g\lambda}$ will have units of $\sqrt{ms^{-2} \times m} = ms^{-1}$, which is therefore dimensionally correct.

A3 wave speed = distance/time = $60/150 = 0.4\,ms^{-1}$.
The periodic time = 9.0 s, giving a frequency, $f = 1/9 = 0.111\,Hz$.
Now $\lambda = v/f = 0.4/0.111 = 3.6\,m$.

***examiner's* note** Information is given indirectly in question 3; you need to do simple calculations to find wave speed.

Phase difference and path difference

Q1 Give three ways in which phase difference might be expressed.

Q2 In terms of wavelength, what are the path differences corresponding to the following phase differences (given in radians): 0, $\pi/2$, π, $3\pi/2$, 2π?

Q3 A compression wave of frequency 400 Hz travels at a speed of 6000 m s^{-1} along a long, metal railway line. What is the phase difference between points on the rail that are 7.5 m apart?

ANSWERS

A1 • As an angle (e.g. $\pi/2$ radians)
   • As the distance along a wave profile (or path difference)
   • As a time difference along the wave profile

A2 $0, \lambda/4, \lambda/2, 3\lambda/4, \lambda$

A3 wavelength = v/f = 6000/400 = 15.0 m. Since the path difference
   = 7.5 m, this represents 7.5/15.0 = $\frac{1}{2}$ × wavelength, which is
   equivalent to π radians.

***examiner's* note** Phase difference = $(2\pi/\lambda)$ × path difference.

Electromagnetic waves

Q1 Describe an electromagnetic (EM) wave in terms of electric and magnetic vectors.

Q2 Give four characteristics of EM waves.

Q3 Red monochromatic laser light of wavelength 780 nm is used to read the ridges in compact discs. Calculate the frequency of the red laser light.

ANSWERS

A1 An oscillating electric field E and an oscillating magnetic field B, perpendicular to each other and to the direction of travel of the wave

A2 • They are all transverse waves
   • They all travel at the same speed in a vacuum (the speed of light)
   • They can be plane polarised
   • They are undeviated by electric and magnetic fields

A3 $c = f\lambda$, giving $f = c/\lambda = (3 \times 10^8)/(780 \times 10^{-9}) = 3.85 \times 10^{14}\,\text{Hz}$

examiner's note Only in a vacuum does light travel at c. $1\,\text{nm} = 10^{-9}\,\text{m}$.

Plane polarisation of waves I

Q1 Define plane polarisation.

Q2 How would you distinguish between polarised and unpolarised light?

Q3 Give three uses for plane polarisation.

ANSWERS))

A1 Polarised waves have their electric fields oscillating in one plane only

A2 View the light through a Polaroid. If the brightness remains the same on rotating the Polaroid, then the light is unpolarised. However, if the light appears alternately bright and dark, then the light is polarised.

A3 Sunglasses, stress analysis and optical analysis of solutions (e.g. sugars or amino acids)

***examiner's* note** Polarisation is a property shown only by transverse waves. In question 2, on rotating the analysing Polaroid, 'brightness' is seen every π radians (or 180°).

Plane polarisation of waves II

Q1 Which statement regarding a plane-polarised wave is correct?
A   Only electromagnetic waves can be plane-polarised.
B   Two light beams, plane-polarised in perpendicular directions exhibit small interference effects.
C   Plane-polarised waves are associated with transverse waves only.
D   Plane-polarised waves are transmitted through a Polaroid only if its plane of polarisation is parallel to the axis of polarisation of the Polaroid.

Q2 What is Malus' law?

Q3 A beam of plane-polarised light of intensity $40\,W\,m^{-2}$ passes through Polaroid A then Polaroid B. The characteristic direction of B is perpendicular to the incident beam. If A is oriented at $30°$ to the incident beam, calculate the intensity of the emergent beam from B.

ANSWERS 》

A1 C is correct.

A2 $I = I_0 \cos^2 \theta$, where I_0 = intensity of incident light on a Polaroid,
I = intensity of emergent light from Polaroid when rotated at an
angle θ to the plane of polarisation

A3 In this case, $I_0 = 40\,\text{W}\,\text{m}^{-2}$; $I_1 = 40 \cos^2 30° = 30\,\text{W}\,\text{m}^{-2}$ and
$I_2 = I_1 \cos^2 60° = 7.5\,\text{W}\,\text{m}^{-2}$

examiner's **note** Plane-polarised waves are possible with transverse waves
only. They are polarised in the direction perpendicular to the direction of travel
of the wave and are only entirely extinguished by Polaroids whose characteristic
directions are perpendicular to the direction of polarisation.

Inverse square law I

Q1 Define the intensity of a wave and give its SI unit.

Q2 State the inverse square law and state any assumptions made.

Q3 If sound waves are emitted from a 150 W point source, what is the intensity of the wave (a) 4 m and (b) 8 m from the source?

ANSWERS

A1 Power per unit area; SI unit is $W\,m^{-2}$

A2 $I = P/4\pi R^2$, where R = distance from the source. Assumptions made are point source of waves and no power absorbed in the intervening medium.

A3 (a) $I_4 = 150/4\pi(4)^2 = 0.746\ W\,m^{-2}$
(b) $I_8 = 150/4\pi(8)^2 = 0.187\ W\,m^{-2}$

***examiner's* note** Questions sometimes involve sources having an efficiency less than 100%, in which case the power must be reduced by a certain factor. Other questions can involve calculating the power of a source (e.g. the Sun) from knowledge of the intensity at a given distance (e.g. at the Earth's surface).

Inverse square law II

Q1 The variation in count rate R with distance d between a small radioactive source emitting gamma (γ) radiation and a Geiger–Müller tube is given below. Without plotting a graph, show that the data follow an inverse square law.

R/counts min⁻¹	610	350	215	145
d/cm	15	20	25	30

Q2 If sound waves are emitted from a 150 W point source, what is the intensity 4 m from the source?

Q3 The amplitude of vibration of air molecules 4 m from the source is 50×10^{-6} m. What is the amplitude at 10 m (assuming no energy loss)?

ANSWERS ❯❯

A1 At 15 cm, $k = 610 \times (15)^2 = 137\,250$ min^{-1} cm^{-1}

At 20 cm, $k = 350 \times (20)^2 = 140\,000$ min^{-1} cm^{-1}

At 25 cm, $k = 215 \times (25)^2 = 134\,375$ min^{-1} cm^{-1}

At 30 cm, $k = 145 \times (30)^2 = 130\,500$ min^{-1} cm^{-1}

Since k is approximately constant, it may be assumed that the inverse law is obeyed.

A2 $I_4 = 150/4\pi(4)^2 = 0.746$ W m^{-2}

A3 The intensity 10 m from the source, $I_{10} = 150/4\pi(10)^2 = 0.119$ W m^{-2}. Intensity I is proportional to the square of the amplitude of vibration A, $I = kA^2$, so $0.746 = kA^2 = k(50 \times 10^{-6})^2$ and $0.119 = kx^2$, which gives $x^2/(50 \times 10^{-6})^2 = 0.119/0.746$ giving $x = 20 \times 10^{-6}$ m.

examiner's note In question 1, a graph of R vs $1/d^2$ would be a straight line passing through the origin if the inverse square law is obeyed.

Wavefronts I

Q1 (a) What are wavefronts? (b) How may they be illustrated in practice?

Q2 What is the significance of a wavefront?

Q3 What is the relationship between a wavefront and an associated ray?

ANSWERS

A1 (a) A wavefront is a line or surface on which all particles are vibrating in phase

(b) Throwing a pebble into a pond causes a disturbance (point source); the wavefronts (circular ripples) then move outwards

A2 It shows how energy travels from one place to another in a medium

A3 A ray is a line giving the direction of the wave, and it is at 90° to the wavefronts

***examiner's* note** The example chosen in question 1(b) is two-dimensional. Wavefronts from a point source are spheres that are centred on the point source, e.g. the Sun radiating heat and light to the Solar System. This has links with the inverse square law. At large distances from the point source, wavefronts become plane and the rays parallel.

Wavefronts II

Q1 State and explain Huygens' principle.

Q2 The diagram shows circular wavefronts that are being refracted at a plane boundary between shallow water and deep water. Which part of the diagram represents deep water?

Q3 For the same situation, find the ratio of the wave speeds in deep and shallow water. Explain your calculation.

ANSWERS

A1 Every point on an existing wavefront becomes a new or 'secondary' centre of disturbance. In practice, we fix on one position of the wavefront and to find where it will be after t s, we suppose that each point on the wavefront acts as a source, sending out fresh waves, all in phase of radius vt, where v is the wave speed in an homogeneous medium.

A2 Right-hand side

A3 $1.5 : 1$

***examiner's* note** Huygens' principle is especially valuable for drawing the new wavefront when light travels from one medium to another. In question 2, the wavefronts are further apart on the right-hand side of PQRS, so the wavelength is larger. In question 3, since frequency is constant, it follows that the wave speed is higher by the ratio of the wavelengths (3 mm to 2 mm).

Principle of superposition

Q1 State the principle of superposition.

Q2 What is meant by interference?

Q3 In terms of wavelength, what are the conditions for:
(a) constructive interference
(b) destructive interference?

ANSWERS ❯❯

A1 The resultant displacement at any point is the sum of the separate displacements due to the two waves

A2 Interference occurs when two waves of the same wavelength from a coherent source interact to produce maxima or minima

A3 (a) Path difference = 0, λ, 2λ, 3λ etc. or a whole number of wavelengths
(b) Path difference = $\lambda/2$, $3\lambda/2$, $5\lambda/2$ etc. or an odd number of half wavelengths

***examiner's* note** The principle applies to all types of wave and for more than two waves. Coherent sources are in phase (or have a constant phase difference).

Stationary (standing) waves I

Q1 What is the definition of a stationary (standing) wave?

Q2 How is energy transferred in (a) a progressive wave and (b) a standing wave?

Q3 Define (a) nodes and (b) antinodes in standing waves.

ANSWERS

A1 A stationary wave is one in which the wave profile does not move, but is located in one position

A2 (a) Energy is transferred from one point to another
(b) Energy is stored on the wave because of the vibration of the particles

A3 (a) Positions of zero displacement
(b) Positions of maximum displacement

***examiner's* note** A stationary wave results when two waves that are travelling in opposite directions and that have the same speed and frequency and approximately the same amplitude are superimposed.

Stationary (standing) waves II

Q1 Describe an experiment to demonstrate stationary waves.

Q2 A student oscillates one end of a rope, 1 m long; the other end is attached horizontally to a wall. She notes that the nodes are 0.4 m apart. If the speed of the waves in the rope is 80 cm s^{-1}, what is the frequency with which the student is moving the free end?

Q3 A small source S of electromagnetic waves is placed some distance from a plane metal reflector M. A detector D, moving between S and M along the line normal to the reflector, detects the average distance between successive minima to be 1.5 cm. Calculate the frequency of the source S if the speed of electromagnetic waves in air is 3×10^8 m s^{-1}.

ANSWERS

A1 A vibrating tuning fork is held over the end of a long, narrow, vertical tube filled with water. A tap at the bottom allows water to flow slowly out of the tube. A sound of loud intensity is heard when the water reaches certain levels because a standing wave has been set up in the tube.

A2 Nodes are 0.4 m apart, giving $\lambda = 2 \times 0.4 = 0.8$ m.
Now, $f = 0.8/0.8 = 1$ Hz.

A3 Nodes are 1.5 cm apart, giving $\lambda = 2 \times 1.5 = 3.0$ cm.
$f = (3.0 \times 10^8)/3.0 \times 10^{-2} = 10^{10}$ Hz.

***examiner's* note** Sound is reflected from the water surface (always a node); open ends of tubes are always antinodes. Resonant lengths correspond to $\lambda/4$, $3\lambda/4$, $5\lambda/4$ etc.

Stationary (standing) waves III

Q1 A loudspeaker emitting a note of 1056 Hz was placed at the open end of a tube of adjustable length. It was found that adjacent resonances were heard when the length was 46.8 cm and 62.4 cm. Calculate the speed of sound in air.

Q2 At points on the straight line between two successive displacement nodes in a stationary sound wave:

A   particle velocities are equal
B   pressure amplitude is constant
C   oscillations are out of phase
D   the velocities of adjacent particles are out of phase
E   the accelerations of adjacent particles are in phase

ANSWERS

A1 The first position is at $\lambda/4$ and the second is at $3\lambda/4$, so the distance between them is $\lambda/2 = (62.4 - 46.8) = 15.6\,\text{cm}$. This gives $\lambda = 31.2\,\text{cm}$. Since $v = f\lambda$, this gives $v = 0.312 \times 1056 = 329\,\text{m s}^{-1}$.

A2 E is the correct answer.

***examiner's* note** In question 2, the particle velocities and amplitudes will be different (answer A is incorrect). Answers C and D are incorrect since all particles between nodes are moving in phase.

Young's slits experiment

Q1 (a) In Young's slits experiment, what is the equation relating wavelength (λ), slit–screen distance (D), slit separation (s) and fringe width (x)? (b) Give typical values for D and s for visible light.

Q2 What are the important features about the (visible) light sources for the successful viewing of bright and dark fringes in Young's slits experiment?

Q3 Two coherent radio transmitters A and B, 200 m apart, transmit at a frequency of 100 MHz. A straight road running parallel to AB passes within 4 km of A and B at its nearest point O. Calculate the distance between maximum signals along the road, passing O.

ANSWERS >>

A1 (a) $\lambda = xs/D$

(b) D should be 0.5–1.0 m; s should be less than 1 mm

A2 Sources should be coherent and monochromatic

A3 Wavelength of radio waves $= c/f = (3.0 \times 10^8)/(100 \times 10^6) = 3.0$ m. Then, $\lambda = xs/D$, giving $x = \lambda D/s = (3.0 \times 4000)/(200) = 60$ m.

***examiner's* note** You may need to estimate s and D in a similar way for sound or microwaves — simply use the equation and replace with suitable wavelengths. In question 2, the two light sources should also have equal intensities.

Diffraction

Q1 Define diffraction.

Q2 What condition must be met for diffraction effects to be at a maximum?

Q3 Explain (a) why you can hear but you cannot see around a corner and (b) why you can still pick up a signal on a transistor radio even if a hill blocks the direct route from the transmitter.

ANSWERS

A1 The interference of waves from sources on the same wavefront, which are coherent

A2 The gap through which the wave passes should equal the wavelength of the wave

A3 (a) The wavelength of sound is of the same order of magnitude as the gap (doors, corridors, windows etc.), whereas the wavelength of light is much smaller, so it undergoes minimum diffraction

(b) Long-wave and medium-wave radio waves will diffract around a hill

***examiner's* note** A simpler definition is 'the spreading of waves after they pass through small openings (or round small obstacles)'. VHF waves (used for FM radio) and UHF waves (used for television) have shorter wavelengths and are diffracted only slightly by hills. For good reception for these waves, you normally need a straight path from the transmitter to your radio or television aerial.

Diffraction grating

Q1 State the equation relating the angle between the *n*th order maximum and incident beam for a diffraction grating.

Q2 What is the effect on a diffraction pattern if a finer grating is used?

Q3 A diffraction grating consists of 4000 lines, spread over a distance of 1 cm. If the grating is placed on a spectrometer and illuminated normally with light of wavelength 400 nm, how many fringes can be observed by the telescope?

ANSWERS

A1 $d \sin \theta = n\lambda$, where d = slit distance of grating, λ = wavelength of light, θ = angle between incident and diffracted beam and n = order of the line.

A2 Sharper fringes are obtained, which are further apart.

A3 The largest order fringe corresponds to $\theta = 90°$ and hence $n = d/\lambda = 6$.

***examiner's* note** The same principle is used in X-ray diffraction, in which case d is of the order of inter-atomic or inter-ionic spacing and wavelengths are in the order of 10^{-10} m.

Wave–particle duality

Q1 What is meant by wave–particle duality?

Q2 (a) Which two prominent seventeenth-century scientists subscribed to (i) particle theory and (ii) wave theory? (b) Which famous twentieth-century scientist rejected quantum physics?

Q3 State the de Broglie equation. Calculate the de Broglie wavelength of a snooker ball of mass 60 g moving at 2.0 m s⁻¹. Comment on your answer. (Planck constant = 6.63×10^{-34} J s)

ANSWERS

A1 Matter and radiation have both wave-like and particle-like properties

A2 (a) Newton supported particle theory; Huygens supported wave theory

(b) Albert Einstein rejected quantum physics

A3 de Broglie wavelength $\lambda = h/p$, where h = Planck constant and p = momentum of particle. $\lambda = h/p = (6.63 \times 10^{-34})/(0.06 \times 2) = 5.5 \times 10^{-33}$ m. It is so small (well below the wavelength of gamma radiation) that it has no physical significance.

***examiner's* note** The de Broglie wavelength has most meaning for subatomic particles at relativistic speeds.

Photoelectric effect

Q1 (a) Describe an experiment to demonstrate the photoelectric effect. (b) What does this experiment illustrate about the nature of light?

Q2 State Einstein's photoelectric equation and use it to obtain an equation relating maximum kinetic energy, work function and energy of the incoming photon.

Q3 What is meant by the stopping potential?

ANSWERS

A1 (a) Shine ultraviolet light onto a cleaned zinc plate on a negatively charged gold-leaf electroscope. The leaves collapse. This shows that electrons were emitted from the metal surface.

(b) The photoelectric effect does not occur if light below the threshold frequency is used, irrespective of intensity. This contradicts wave theory — waves of higher amplitude ought to have greater energy.

A2 $E = hf$, where h = the Planck constant. $E_k = hf - \phi$

A3 The (negative) potential required just to prevent electron emission from a photon-irradiated metal surface

***examiner's* note** You should be familiar with the experimental result that a plot of maximum kinetic energy E_k (y-axis) against frequency f (x-axis) gives a straight line with a positive gradient h and (negative) intercept, ϕ. Different metals have the same slope, but different ϕ values.

Energy levels and line spectra

Q1 What is meant by the energy levels in an atom?

Q2 (a) What fact about atoms does a line spectrum demonstrate experimentally? (b) Name two alternative pieces of equipment needed to show line spectra.

Q3 In the hydrogen atom, what is the wavelength of the H_α line in the hydrogen spectrum, arising from transition between levels E_3 and E_2 (-2.43×10^{-19} J and -5.45×10^{-19} J respectively)? ($c = 3 \times 10^8$ m s^{-1}, $h = 6.63 \times 10^{-34}$ J s, $e = -1.6 \times 10^{-19}$ C)

ANSWERS 〉〉

A1 An atom has a number of separate electron energy levels, characteristic for a particular atom. An atom cannot have any energy between these levels — energy is said to be 'quantised'.

A2 (a) That there are energy levels in an atom
(b) Glass prism or diffraction grating

A3 $E_3 - E_2 = (-2.43 \times 10^{-19}) - (-5.45 \times 10^{-19}) = hf = hc/\lambda$
∴ $3.02 \times 10^{-19} = (6.63 \times 10^{-34} \times 3 \times 10^8)/\lambda$, giving $\lambda = 659$ nm

***examiner's* note** Bohr's theory of the hydrogen atom gave important new ideas about atoms. Only gaseous atoms give line spectra. The relationship $E = hf = hc/\lambda$ is useful in calculations of this type.

Reflection and refraction at a plane surface

Q1 State the laws of reflection at plane surfaces.

Q2 State the laws of refraction at plane surfaces.

Q3 How does the density of a medium affect (a) the speed, (b) the frequency and (c) the wavelength of a wave travelling in it?

ANSWERS

A1 The incident ray, the reflected ray and the normal at the point of incidence all lie in the same plane. The angle of incidence i = angle of reflection r.

A2 The incident ray, the refracted ray and the normal at the point of incidence all lie in the same plane. For two given media ($\sin i/\sin r$) is constant, where i is the angle of incidence and r is the angle of refraction (Snell's law).

A3 (a) The wave speed is inversely proportional to the density of medium through which it moves

(b) Frequency is independent of the medium

(c) Wavelength will vary inversely with density of the medium

***examiner's* note** The answer to question 3c follows from the answer to question 3b and the equation $c = f\lambda$.

Snell's law and refractive index

Q1 Define refractive index.

Q2 Explain how Snell's law is applied to light passing between two media.

Q3 Explain critical angle and total internal reflection.

ANSWERS)》

A1 Refractive index n = (speed of light in free space/speed of light in medium)

A2 When a ray is refracted from one medium to another, the boundaries being parallel, $n \sin i$ = constant

A3 Total internal reflection can happen only when a ray travelling through a material of higher refractive index reaches the boundary with a material of lower refractive index. It occurs for any angle of incidence equal to or greater than the critical angle, C.

examiner's note For rays passing from medium 1 to medium 2, the interface being parallel: $n_1 \sin i_1 = n_2 \sin i_2$. Also, $\sin C = 1/n$.

Total internal reflection and critical angle

Q1 Name two types of optical fibre.

Q2 Describe (a) the uses and (b) the advantages of using optical fibres.

Q3 If the core of an optical fibre has a refractive index of 1.52, and the cladding has a refractive index of 1.48, calculate the critical angle at the interface.

ANSWERS ▶▶

A1 Monomode and multimode fibres

A2 (a) Telecommunications networks (carrying telephone messages), cable television and internet communications

(b) Since light has a high frequency, optical fibres can carry much more data than a current in a cable of comparable size

A3 $n \sin i$ = constant, giving $n_1 \sin C = n_2 \sin 90°$, i.e. $\sin C = (n_2/n_1)$; thus, $\sin C = (1.48/1.52) = 0.974$, giving $C = 76.8°$

examiner's note A monomode fibre has a very narrow core of diameter about $5\,\mu m$ or less; a multimode fibre has a core of relatively large diameter, such as $50\,\mu m$. This is a step index multimode fibre. Graded index multimode fibres are also available in which there is no noticeable boundary between core and cladding.

Refraction through lenses

Q1 Define the focal length and power of a converging lens.

Q2 Give the equation relating the object distance u, image distance v and the focal length of a lens.

Q3 The graph shows how the magnification m of a thin converging lens varied with image distance v. What is the focal length of the lens?

A b/c B b/ca C bc/a

D ab/c E c/b

ANSWERS

A1 The focal length f is the distance between the principal axis and the focus. The power of a lens with focal length f (m) is $1/f$, the lens power being given in dioptres (D).

A2 The 'real-is-positive' lens equation states that $1/f = 1/u + 1/v$, distances being measured from the pole, along the principal axis. A + sign is given to real object and image distances and a − sign is given to virtual object and image distances.

A3 Option E is the correct response

***examiner's* note** Using the real-is-positive sign convention, $1/f = 1/u + 1/v$. Multiplying by v gives $v/u = (v/f) - 1$. Magnification $m = v/u$, so $m = (v/f) - 1$. Plotting m against v gives a straight line with gradient $= 1/f$.

Sum over paths: theory

Q1 Which equation is used to calculate the frequency of rotation of a photon phasor?

Q2 How are two phasor arrows combined to give a resultant?

Q3 How will a point appear if the probability for a light photon is zero there?

ANSWERS

A1 $f = E_k/h$, where f = frequency, E_k = kinetic energy and h = the Planck constant.

A2 The resultant phasor arrow is found by adding the final phasor position for each path.

A3 Darkness

***examiner's* note** Vectors are added tip to tail, just like normal vector addition. The brightness of an area depends on the probability of a photon arriving there.

Sum over paths: applications

Q1 Explain reflection in a plane mirror using 'sum over paths'.

Q2 Explain refraction using 'sum over paths'.

Q3 Using 'sum over paths', explain how light is focused by a convex lens.

ANSWERS ▶▶

A1 The rule says that a photon will take every possible path. We need to find the final position of the photon's phasor for every possible path and sum the final phasors to calculate the resultant.

A2 When light travels in water, it slows down, but its frequency stays the same. The photons still have the same energy and their phasors have the same amplitude and frequency of rotation.

A3 The paths towards the edges of the lens are longer than those through the centre. The time taken for light to travel each path is the same because there is more glass in the central part of the lens. This increases the time it takes for light to travel the shorter paths between the object and the focus.

***examiner's* note** The final phasors for the longest, slowest paths near the ends of the mirror 'curl up', almost cancelling themselves out. Lenses add curvature to wavefronts by refraction.

Digital imaging

Q1 Define the bit and the byte.

Q2 How can (a) the contrast and (b) the brightness of an image be improved?

Q3 State the Laplace rule. Explain how it is used.

ANSWERS ▶▶

A1 A single binary digit is called a bit; a group of eight binary digits is called a byte.

A2 (a) Multiplying by a fixed value improves contrast (b) Adding a fixed positive value makes the image brighter

A3 The Laplace rule is used to find edges. To apply the rule, multiply a pixel by four, then subtract the value of the pixels immediately above, below, to the left and to the right of it.

***examiner's* note** The binary system uses only two digits (0 and 1).

Multiplying also increases the brightness. However, adding does not change the contrast.

The result of the Laplace rule is that any pixel not on the edge goes black, leaving just the edges.

Analogue and digital signals

Q1 Explain the difference between analogue and digital signals.

Q2 Give three advantages of using digital signals over analogue ones.

Q3 An analogue signal contains frequencies at 50 Hz, 250 Hz, 150 Hz and 125 Hz. What is the minimum sampling rate that should be used when digitising this signal?

ANSWERS

A1 Digital signals are represented by binary numbers; analogue signals vary continuously.

A2 They are resistant to the effects of noise; easy to process using computers; can be used to represent different types of data in the same way, e.g. images or sound.

A3 500 Hz

***examiner's* note** Another benefit of digital signals is the fact that they can be sent, received and reproduced more easily than analogue signals owing to their limited number of values.

Minimum sampling rate = 2 × maximum frequency = 2 × 250 = 500 samples per second.

Signal spectra and bandwidth

Q1 Explain the meaning of (a) the spectrum and (b) the bandwidth of a signal?

Q2 What are carrier waves and why are they used?

Q3 A telephone system samples the voice 5000 times a second and converts this into an eight-bit digital signal. (a) What is the rate of transmission for bits in this system? (b) How many bytes can be sent per second?

ANSWERS ❭❭

A1 (a) The spectrum is the frequencies that make up a signal (b) The bandwidth is the range of frequencies within a signal.

A2 The carrier wave is the high-frequency radio wave that transmits the signal.

A3 (a) Rate of transmission = samples per second × bits per sample = 5000 × 8 = 40 000 bits per second (b) 1 byte = 8 bits, giving 40 000 bits per second = 5 000 bytes per second.

***examiner's* note** All radio stations are assigned a particular carrier frequency on which to transmit their signals. Carrier frequencies in a local area must be different in order that they do not interfere with each other.

Errors of observation and their treatment

Q1 Explain the difference between random and systematic errors.

Q2 (a) Give one example of each type of error.
(b) Describe one way of minimising the uncertainty for both random and systematic errors.

Q3 A student, wishing to find the density of a cube, measures its mass and the mean length of the sides. Values of (100 ± 4) g and (5.0 ± 0.1) cm are obtained. How should the student best quote the value for density?

ANSWERS ▶▶

A1 Random errors occur when repeated measurements of the same quantity give different values. Systematic error refers to an effect that influences all measurements of a particular quantity equally.

A2 (a) Random errors come from the inability of any instrument to give infinitely accurate answers. Systematic errors may arise from lack of calibration. (b) Random errors are minimised by averaging a number of observations. Systematic errors are avoided or minimised by calibrating or zeroing instruments.

A3 density = mass/volume. We add percentage errors to obtain maximum possible error. So, $\Delta\rho = \Delta m + \Delta V = \Delta m + 3\Delta L$.
Since $V = L^3$, the error in L is tripled. $\Delta\rho = (4/100) + 3(0.1/5.0) = 0.04 + 0.06 = 0.100$ or 10%.
Since $100/125 = 0.80$ and 10% of 0.80 = 0.08, the best quote is $(0.80 \pm 0.08)\,\mathrm{g\,cm^{-3}}$.

***examiner's* note** It is sometimes difficult to distinguish between the two types of error and many errors are a combination of the two types.